Making It Better for Boys in Schools, Families and Communities

Also available from Network Continuum

Breaking Through the Barriers to Boys' Achievement – Gary Wilson

Pocket PAL: Boys and Writing – Steve Bowkett

Pocket PAL: Raising Boys' Achievement – Gary Wilson

Raising Boys' Achievement – Jon Pickering

Available from Continuum

Managing Boys' Behaviour – Tabatha Rayment

Making It Better for Boys in Schools, Families and Communities

Ali McClure

network
continuum

Continuum International Publishing Group
Network Continuum
The Tower Building   80 Maiden Lane, Suite 704
11 York Road   New York, NY 10038
SE1 7NX

www.networkcontinuum.co.uk
www.continuumbooks.com

British Library Cataloguing-in-Publication Data
A catalogue record for this book is available from the British Library.

ISBN: 9781855394353 (paperback)

Library of Congress Cataloguing-in-Publication Data
The Publisher has applied for CIP data.

Typeset by Newgen Imaging Systems Pvt Ltd, Chennai, India
Printed and bound in Great Britain by MPG Books, Cornwall
Illustrations by Kerry Ingham

To
Chris, Josh, Callum, Sam, Peter and Peter,
the very special boys in my life.

Acknowledgements

Heartfelt thanks to all my family and friends, to all the parents, teachers and early years professionals who have believed in me and the 'Making It Better for Boys' mission from the beginning.

Thanks is also due to the following people:

David Leggett; Bridget Gibbs; Sue Hedges; Anne Sarakinis and Women FM; Sallianne Robinson; Mary Crowley and Parenting UK; Chris Lane; David Lloyd Leisure Clubs; Liz Lander; Sally Royds; Becci Murphy; Steve Biddulph; Candida Hunt; Margot Sunderland; Anne Rawlings; Sue Palmer; Chris Lane; Clare Catt; Caroline Cave; Alison Archibald; Amanda Rushton; Arie de Geus; Kate Long; Garry Tinsley; Bill Lucas; Janita Chohan; Simon Ward; Lucy Creegan; Nick Giovanelli and HACSG; Stephanie Ward; Celia Armour; Michael Gurian; Stephanie van Goozen; Tom Daly; Ivy Bird; Shirley McClure; Mary Jane Taylor; Fiona Taylor and SPES; Dr. Mary Bousted; Amanda Fowler; Suzanne Hoddinott; Bernie Tonge; Bridget Lincoln; Tim Benson and Homestart; Clive Biles; Derek Smith; John Marshall; Julie Skelton; Karen Porter; Boyd Llelliott.

National Childbirth Trust; Sallianne and Friends Day Nursery; Greenacres Preschool; Windhams Nursery School; Stoughton Infant and Nursery School; Ripley Infant School; Holy Trinity Junior School; St Nicolas Primary School; Northmead Junior School; Wood Street Infant School; Tillingbourne Junior School; The Mount Primary School; Kings College Guildford; Kingston University London; Roehampton University; University of Surrey.

Contents

Introduction:
Making it better for boys

This book is clearly and unapologetically about boys. The issues it raises are crucial to the development and understanding of boys, where each one of us in schools, families and communities can make a real difference. Together we can make life better for boys and for girls, in fact, for all children whatever their needs or abilities. The knock-on effects of our actions will bring positive and profound changes for children, parents, schools and communities in the twenty-first century.

In a busy international airport earlier this year a man in his thirties offered to share his seat with my five-year-old son. Why should this be so incredible? What relevance is this to boys in our schools and families? Ask yourself . . . would you see a British male in a British airport do this? I suspect not.

In Britain in the late twentieth century and early twenty-first, many people have been taught a culture of fear and mistrust, especially of the male population. Walk down any High Street. Look around and consider how many men you see that you would trust. Is it more likely that you would be suspicious of men, of the Big Issue seller, the shop assistant on his break, the hooded teenager who walks as if the world is against him?

Think of our young boys and teenagers. Are we as a society warm to them?

Boys are berated for their behaviour, spurned and distanced from us. It seems to be acceptable for politicians, the police, family members, teachers and even strangers to comment on boys' behaviour without questioning the reasons that may be behind their actions.

In schools, boys are frequently seen as the tough option – 'How many boys in that class? That must be hard work!'

I wonder how many education professionals really understand the struggles and fears of boys, the ways they access learning and what underlies the behaviours that are so often seen as inappropriate or antisocial.

Those of us who are parents of boys discover that many people feel the need to commiserate with us, especially if we have more than one.

'You poor thing, how do you cope? Two boys . . . I can't think of anything worse!'

Sadly these are genuine comments and from highly trained and caring professionals who work with boys every day.

Teenaged boys are often labelled 'yobs', 'thugs' or 'louts'. Young boys are often seen branded by the 'labels' on their T-shirts . . . 'Little Monster' or 'Little Monkey'. Labels are more powerful than they would seem. It is no wonder many boys behave the way the labels suggest.

Bad behaviour from boys has become what society expects and for that reason alone many adults in our Western culture avoid sharing their space with young boys . . . they anticipate that their behaviour may be less than pleasant, it may live up to the label!

In Bahrain airport, I was surprised as my son was greeted by many adults and welcomed with a warm smile and a ruffle of his hair. He was, however, unsure as to whether he should take up this offer of a shared seat with a strange man. Back in Britain my son has been instructed not to go with strangers and if ever he were lost he has a clear picture of who to turn to. Is there a man in that picture? Only if he is a police officer or a man in recognized uniform, but it would never be an ordinary man. The people in the picture would more likely be women, perhaps a shopkeeper or a woman with a pushchair but never, never a man!

Isn't it sad that in Britain a caring man, perhaps a father himself is scared to help a child for fear of being accused of inappropriate behaviour or being assaulted? One in eight British men in a recent National Children's Home survey (May 2007) said they would not choose to volunteer to work with children due to fear of being perceived as a paedophile.

How must it feel for a boy to grow up knowing that very soon he will be mistrusted by many, just because he's a man? Boys see the media making headlines of teenagers hurting people, hurting younger children.

'When I'm older I will have to be cool and I might hurt younger children. I don't want to do that' (Sam aged 6).

At what age will he become a person to be feared and avoided? Has it already happened?

The kindness of the gentleman in the airport really prompted me to reflect on national differences in culture and the attitude in Britain and the United States towards boys and men.

From my brief experience it would seem that in Bahrain the following statements hold true:

• men like children and are often kind to them

- men are trusted around children
- children trust men
- other adults trust men
- young boys are seen in a positive light

Sadly, these statements substantially do not hold true in Western society. In Britain there is a national airline that does not let unknown men sit next to children on their flights.

We are living in a blame culture. We cannot smile at someone, touch someone, offer to help or comfort someone, ask for help and let our children be children for fear of accusation and blame or a wrongdoing. From a young age people are encouraged to know their rights and sue if these are violated. With all these rights where are responsibilities and respect?

These issues are huge for everyone in society but particularly for schools. Schools are in the privileged and powerful position to be able to make changes, both to familiar policies and to practices that we may not even realize are damaging our children, especially boys. Schools are now empowered through Every Child Matters, the UNICEF report (2007), the Respect Agenda (Home Office, January 2006) and the Gender Agenda (Gender Equality Duty, April 2007) as the nucleus in the cell of every community.

If we believe in a better future for boys and young men then we must be passionate about being positive about boys. If we engage with parents, professionals and community networks we can pool our passion and make a vital difference. As Anita Roddick of the Body Shop put it so effectively 'If you think you are too small to make a difference try sleeping with a mosquito'.

Throughout the book the underlying message is that we need to work together to make things better. Schools, families and communities need to work as one, sharing the same passion and drive to build a better future for boys and for everyone. The symbols in the key below are used in several chapters with suggested points for action.

Key

Schools

Families

Communities

I believe that the issues facing our boys, men and society today can be overcome through small changes but these changes will be the pebbles in the pond. The ripples will have a steady but dramatic effect on the lives of all boys, the men they grow to be and the families they will ultimately nurture.

The workshop on which this book is based has generated such humbling comments as 'wonderful', 'life-changing', 'saved the life of my teenage son', and each time I have the privilege to share my passion for this subject with people they leave empowered and determined to make changes. I hope this book inspires and empowers you to make changes and to tell others how together we can most definitely 'Make It Better for Boys'.

Part 1
Moulding Twenty-First-Century Men

Equipped to be men

Whenever young boys go out for a walk they come back with 'stuff'. It seems to me that it is nigh on impossible to return without a special rock, stone or stick. Even on a trip to the supermarket they come home with a collection of boxes to make things from. Boys like equipment. They need to build or make and are drawn to the equipment they need. Knives, rope, hammers, tools of every kind seem to have a magnetic pull for boys. It is as if they know innately that they need to prepare for the skills they may need as a man.

Now consider what young boys are given as presents in the twenty-first century. Most toys are made from plastic and often arrive complete. They are usually pre-designed and apart from a few, they frequently only have one function. Boys are still given construction toys and 'meccano' sets but, in contrast, how often are they bought computer games, play consoles, DVDs and other technology especially as they get older. Technology has a crucial part to play in life today but we do need to consider what skills and qualities the technological age encourages in our boys . . . Are these the skills and qualities that will help them grow into confident, effective young men?

If you were to envisage a young boy's journey from child to man, what physical equipment would you give him?

Many of the boxed and marketed toys that boys have these days come with a manual or are marketed through TV advertisements that show how to use them. In schools the curriculum is prescriptive with a manual to tell you how to teach so that your students might achieve certain levels and pass the required tests. Boys are given fewer opportunities in the twenty-first century to be creative, to solve their own problems.

Boys need stuff

The following cartoon suggests just some of what boys might need to be equipped to be men. For the twenty-first century, perhaps the list should also include . . .

computer   bike
money   phone
sat-nav   travel pass
condoms   credit card

However, being equipped to be a man is so much more than tangible equipment. It is, as Steve Biddulph (1998) says, 'Important to know what a good man looks like'.

Good men in the twenty-first century

How many _good_ men do our boys get to spend time with in schools, families and the community today? In our homes many fathers are absent, whether through the fragmentation of families or the demands of work. Children in nurseries and early years settings rarely come across male education and childcare professionals. In schools the workforce is predominantly female and in the community many men are reluctant to get involved with boys because of the blame culture and the demands of day-to-day life. Everyday life seems to be pressured with no time to just stop and to be children, to be boys.

Rather than being in the world of _good_ men, boys are inclined to be engrossed in a virtual world of today's technology. Their heroes are more likely to be in Los Angeles than in their home town; they may even be in an imaginary world, only ever achievable via a screen. Technology is part of our lives and very valuable but we need to teach the playstation generation that technology has its place and to use it wisely. We all need to attend to the real people in our lives rather than the surrogate parents that computers and screens have become, especially for boys.

We live in a vibrant, exciting and often challenging world in the twenty-first century and we need to prepare our boys for this world and to arm them with skills to deal with whatever the world may bring tomorrow. How can we do this? Not just with equipment but with information, skills, good role models, compassion, self-esteem, emotional literacy, physical and mental strength and the confidence and self-belief to put these things into practice.

Of course, we all know that in the twenty-first century men do not simply go out and hunt but do we also know that many of the skills necessary for hunting are still inbuilt into the way our boys' bodies and brains develop? Today, roles for men and women have become much more interchangeable and the importance of both sexes being offered the same opportunities and being treated equally is of great importance. My question is, while recognizing the work that so many women do for boys, how do we ensure that the opportunities for boys to learn to be *good men* are as readily accessible as those for girls to learn how to become good women?

In their formative years, girls spend the vast majority of their time around other females. They have constant opportunities to learn from female role models . . . to learn at first hand how to be a good woman. They are often around younger children and learn the skills of good mothers. They share experiences and talk a great deal about what they are doing.

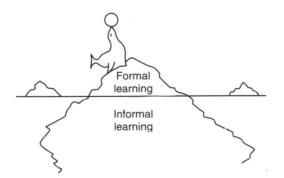

Lucas, (2005) *Discover Your Hidden Talents*. With kind permission.

Learning to be men

In our busy lives, boys have fewer and fewer opportunities to learn from other men . . . to learn how to become a good man. When boys and men are together they frequently share technological activities and talk little. Boys are often around younger children and learn from the women some skills of a parent but, despite the best efforts of the women, how do these boys learn to be fathers, good fathers? How do they observe at first hand the experiences of being a man?

> If we were judged in education and society today on how well we equip our boys for their future as good men the result would be plainly . . . unsatisfactory.

We have made great strides in education over recent years to encourage equality of access to reading, writing, numeracy, science; the academic subjects for both sexes. We still need to go much further by looking at how boys learn in broader terms. Bill Lucas of The Talent Foundation speaking at Surrey University in 2007 suggests that two-thirds of learning is informal . . . beneath the surface, rather like an iceberg.

Skills and qualities

The following list, based on my workshop 'Making It Better for Boys', is far from comprehensive. It shows just how much of what we learn in our lives is about skills. With the right skills, good self-esteem and, importantly, a passion to learn, boys can gain the knowledge they need and make or acquire the tools necessary in order to be 'equipped to be men'.

Skills and qualities boys need to become good men in the twenty-first century

Becoming effective learners	Being passionate about learning
Being creative – finding creative solutions	Being responsible
Finding and keeping good friends	Making good choices
Keeping healthy and strong	Working as a team member
Keeping fit – in mind and body	Overcoming peer and negative pressure
Pursuing healthy pastimes	Being reliable
Finding and keeping a good mate	Planning for the future

Being good with money

Providing food

Questioning things that are wrong

Understanding feelings – their own and those of others

Exploring new things

Enjoying sport

Having time to think, reflect and relax

Managing and channelling stress in appropriate ways

Being a good life partner

Learning to listen

Passing on skills

Communicating with males and females of all ages

Resisting or managing temptation

Making shelter

Making things

Understanding emotions at key stages of life

Being strong or gentle at appropriate times

Knowing when and how to ask for help

Belonging to a community

Fixing things

Living within the rules of being a man

Coping in a crisis

Avoiding unnecessary stress

Having fun today

Challenging bad things

Focusing anger into positive energy

Being committed to partner and family

'Sticking with it' when the going gets tough

Balancing life and work

Being sensitive and caring

Raising great children

Controlling anger

Judging and trialling risk

Showing respect for elders

Taking responsibility

Caring for our planet/ country/community/ home

Community responsibility

Self-defence and appropriate attack

Learning when and who it is appropriate to challenge

Overcoming challenges

Concentration

Commitment

Staying power – persistence

Losing within a supportive environment

Competing in appropriate supportive environments

Relaxing

2 What are boys good at? – schools, families and communities come together

What are boys good at?

Believe in boys. This is something we all need to do whether we care for boys in schools, in families, in early years or in communities. It is so easy to be affected by the media and other people about how terrible boys are. Boys are far from terrible. I am blessed to have three wonderful, individual sons . . . three different sizes but also, you could say, three different styles. All of us who care about boys know that no two are the same yet there are certain things that most boys are typically good at.

> Boys are far from terrible.

What do *you* believe boys are good at? This is such a powerful question it may be useful to raise it as part of a training session. When we know what boys do well we must use this information wisely. In schools we need to use it to empower us, to seize and embrace the exciting opportunities we have, not just for boys, but for our extended schools and our local families and communities.

Extended services . . . how can this make it better for boys?

Extended services, based on Every Child Matters and the Children Act 2004, finally give us a licence to value all the parts of a child's life. For the first time, schools have been given the key to shaping our boys' futures.

Simply put, by 2010 schools have to be able to offer, at the school or locally access to:

- high-quality childcare for school-aged children from 8 a.m. to 6 p.m.
- a varied menu of activities, clubs etc.

- parenting support including parenting programmes, other children's services and family learning sessions
- swift and easy referral to specialist support services
- wider community access including adult learning

This is a powerful key carrying responsibility to build positive futures. Extended schools have been tasked with bringing together families, early years, social services, health, sport, community . . . the list goes on as far as you choose to take it, as far as you and the families in your community want it to go.

Currently, as teachers, parents and members of local communities, we are working as individual strands of thread, all doing our best for boys but often feeling the strain. We need to bond together, to become intertwined with all the people who can make a difference to the lives of boys. We will then be as a strong rope. If we pull together we can make all the parts of boys' lives work in harmony. Instead of vulnerable strands we will have a powerful force to build a positive future through Extended Services.

We need to empower all involved to really believe in and act for boys. It will require communication, cooperation, commitment and community to make this happen. Take a good pen and write each of these words by hand. See how easily they flow and how smoothly they are joined together. This is how I believe the best extended services will flow, seamlessly.

Parents, Adults, Children, Communities and Teachers (PACCT) working together offers such potential (Chapter 11), it is the responsibility of every single person involved to make it a success. It is such an exciting time. If we drive forward believing in boys, then by 2010 we can really make a difference. We will most certainly be 'Making It Better for Boys'.

Teachers

Gary Wilson in *Breaking through Barriers to Boys' Achievement* has a fabulous list of what teachers like about teaching boys. He talks about things such as getting stuck in, their sense of humour, being lively, giving it a go. There are many great things about teaching boys. I wonder if the teachers among us have considered the extent of our responsibility, our privilege and our influence?

I was guilty of breathing a sigh of relief when 'Luke' didn't show up for school.

Boys spend more of their waking hours with teachers than with any other adults, including their parents. As a teacher for many years I consider this responsibility to be daunting, especially as a female teacher, who in the years I was teaching full time had shamefully little understanding of boys, how they learn and behave. I was guilty, as so many teachers are, of breathing a sigh of relief when 'Luke' didn't show up for school. I wonder how welcomed Luke felt in my class and whether my feelings passed on?

If we are going to be successful as PACCT or extended schools we need to ensure everyone feels welcome. I laughed and learned when I first heard this quote by a wise woman called Eleanor Mumford 'The art of hospitality is making someone feel at home . . . even when you wish they were!' We are not talking about homes here but surely, if children spend so long in schools we owe it to them and to everyone who enters our schools to make them feel at home, at ease, offer them hospitality, to make them feel welcome, especially at the times we least feel like it.

A smile and a 'Hello Luke' as you pass him in the corridor cost nothing and you would be amazed at the difference it makes. Members of the community need to feel welcome and *all* members of the school community to be welcoming. We need to make them feel that this school is a place they can always come . . . that they belong.

A policy for Respect and Relationships is a real asset here, raising issues and discussion among staff, parents and children that make a huge difference to so much of school, family and community life.

> A smile and a 'Hello Luke' as you pass him in the corridor cost nothing and you would be amazed at the difference it makes.

At the Mount School they live this philosophy. They have fabulous relationships with children and adults alike; they are particularly successful in involving dads and other good men. People feel they are cared for in this school. I asked Nikki Gray head of the Children's Centre about behaviour challenges and bullying to be told, 'Our children talk to us quickly. They trust us and know we will get things sorted. We hardly have any bullying.'

> If I took trouble to spend time with 'Luke' as an individual and talk to him a little of myself as a person I then had to spend far less time 'telling him off'.

As my career progressed I gradually learnt that if I got to know 'Luke', what he was passionate about and what he was really good at I could nurture that and help him progress. If I took trouble to spend time with 'Luke' as an individual and talk to him a little of myself as a person I then had to spend far less time 'telling him off', 'reprimanding him' and dealing with the behaviours rather than the child. We can complain that we have too little time or too many children in our classes. This is so often true, but hold out for the value of this human approach and maybe we will even get classes sized down to a manageable, more human 24 pupils. The benefits would soon outweigh the costs.

When I am working within Initial Teacher Training so much focus is placed on the National Curriculum, the literacy and numeracy strategies there is hardly a moment in the jam-packed course to value relationships with children, especially challenging ones, particularly boys. The new Professional Standards for Teachers does address this but it is no wonder that many teachers are so focused on planning, assessment, SATS and results that they do not see the wood for the trees. If we motivate and inspire boys they will need so much less behaviour management; our lives will be less stressful and our calm confidence will feed back to them. Again boys will be able to be boys, to enjoy school, to be children. Teachers will once again love their jobs.

> If we motivate and inspire boys they will need so much less behaviour management. Our lives will be less stressful and our calm confidence will feed back to them.

'Where is the Fairy Godmother to wave the magic wand?' I hear you ask.

I am no Fairy Godmother but I firmly believe that if we embrace families and communities with enthusiasm, passion and commitment then it will make life better . . . for all of us who care about boys and for boys themselves. We are all in this game together.

Points for Action – What Are Boys Good At?

- Spend time with boys to get to know them as individuals.
- Ensure that everyone is welcome in your school. Make them feel at home . . . even when you wish they were!
- Know what boys are good at in order to motivate and inspire them.
- Embrace families and communities with enthusiasm and commitment . . . establish a Respect and Relationships policy.
- We need to get all the strands working together to become one strong rope.

Physical activity – more than simply sport

Watch any sport, live or screened and the vast proportion of successful players will be male. Many boys gravitate to sport. Many find it impossible to walk past a ball without kicking it. If we take this skill as something to build on it offers us such opportunities for social skills, negotiation, winning humbly or losing graciously. It helps us introduce some competition, handled appropriately to maintain self-esteem. We need to be particularly sensitive here with those boys to whom sport does not come easily (Chapter 11). For boys particularly, a well-matched sport can help them to develop the gross motor skills – the foundation essential for successful progress to fine motor and access so much learning. It is no wonder that aid agencies refer to 'The power of the ball'.

Many sports involve working as teams. Boys are good at working in teams if there is a respected leader who has earned his position and if the team has a shared purpose. Without a purpose teams can turn into forums for competition and rivalry between the members.

Boys just need to move

Boys whether into sports or not, simply need to move (Chapter 7). However many schools that build on this certainly make things better for the boys in their care and for all around them. Tillingbourne Junior School has fun, physical exercise for all staff and children every morning before school. St Nicolas Primary School break up their morning with a whole school 'wake and shake'. Both of these are fun and are broadly based on Brain Gym. They make a world of difference to the learning, concentration and behaviour that follows. Many of the best schools incorporate brain gym into regular breaks within lessons. One of my favourites is a teacher who overcomes the 'Friday afternoon blues' at his secondary school by playing music from The Benny Hill Show and encouraging his class to move around and have fun. The children have great respect for him and the lessons run much smoothly after a little activity, even on Friday afternoons.

Target sports

Target sports are an area of strength for most boys. Not only is their shoulder musculature built differently to that of girls (this could explain why I am still a 'girly thrower') but they are programmed to look ahead at targets, rather as they would if they were hunting (one of the reasons that boys are drawn to computers and frequently suffer from 'screen suction'). If channelled, this strength can be a powerful tool in the classroom or outdoors, using targets in all kinds of subjects.

I was observing a fabulous infant PE lesson at Ripley Infant School. The children were being taught how to throw a beanbag. One little boy got distracted as there was a workman on a roof in his field of vision. Instead of telling him off, this talented teacher encouraged the boy to focus on the roofer and aim his beanbag at him. Luckily the roofer was a little distance away!

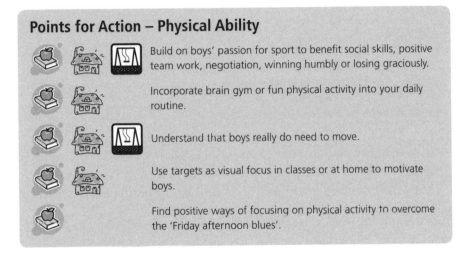

Points for Action – Physical Ability

Build on boys' passion for sport to benefit social skills, positive team work, negotiation, winning humbly or losing graciously.

Incorporate brain gym or fun physical activity into your daily routine.

Understand that boys really do need to move.

Use targets as visual focus in classes or at home to motivate boys.

Find positive ways of focusing on physical activity to overcome the 'Friday afternoon blues'.

Bigger and better

Being seen to be bigger and better than the rest in pretty much all they do is important to boys. They will act out, challenging, peers or adults, if they feel they have a chance of winning, if they feel they are bigger, stronger, faster. They need to feel they are the 'top dog'. Their role play is often about heroes or battles and frequently very physical or noisy. It is also frequently about how they are the strongest and best or how they caught the biggest fish. The flip side of this also means that they have delicate egos and are extremely sensitive to criticism. They are reluctant to ask for help, especially in front of others.

Whether at school or at home it is also crucial that we remember to give specific and authentic praise. It really helps with boys' self-esteem, confidence and emotional literacy if we follow the acronym SPADE...

Specific	'Well done' can be dismissive and confusing. 'What did I do well?' Be specific about the things your boy has done well.
Proud	Be proud of your boys and make the praise personally from you. Start your praise with 'I'. . . I feel really proud when . . . Praise them not only to their face but let them hear that you talk about them proudly to others. (Beware of bruising their 'street cred' when praising teenagers in front of mates.)
Authentic	Never give false praise. Boys see right through it and can find it patronizing. Always be genuine when you praise them.
Descriptive	Describe what you like about his action. 'I loved the way you walked in so calmly.' This helps build up his emotional vocabulary.
Emotional	Just as we calmly express our emotions through tone of voice and expression when we criticize boys, so should we be expressive and show appropriate emotion when praising them. (Remember to be respectful to boys and, if constructive criticism is necessary then do it quietly, calmly and ideally away from his peer group.)

If we ignore a boy or only give him negative feedback he will respond accordingly.

'If he can't be the best at being good he'll be the best at being the worst' (Freed et al.).

Taking risks

Boys are good at taking risks and this is an important part of them testing out their growing bodies. We must allow for risk taking, within safe bounds, both at home and at school. The curriculum currently discourages teachers or pupils from taking risks. It encourages conformity and small achievable tasks. Although these are valuable, sometimes boys do better if given a big challenge. They will see the purpose of developing the skills and gaining the knowledge to help them achieve the goal they are aiming for.

We need to be acutely aware of this when organizing our teaching in sets or streams. We may be taking boys on in carefully planned steps but do we give them the opportunity to reach for the big challenge? Sets can put teacher-imposed ceilings on what children can achieve and give children, especially in lower sets, labels to achieve to. Many Scandinavian countries do not allow grouping by ability.

If we choose to use sets then all children must have opportunities for investigation and open-ended challenges that will stretch their abilities, helping children and teachers to achieve much more. Literacy and numeracy sets need an injection of vitality and purpose. They are in danger of stagnating, the lessons and the teachers alike.

If a boy is asked to design a raft that will float, even a small one, the value of how to measure, do experiments and investigate buoyancy has much more meaning for him than learning slowly and steadily about the little steps along the way. He is much more likely to stay engaged and focused if he can see where he is heading.

Mini enterprise is fabulous for giving children big challenges and allowing them real vehicles for their own creativity; after all risk taking is a form of creativity. We often think of mini enterprise as a secondary activity but I suggest it is never too soon to start. Every spring I would 'poison the parents' (studying and creating our own brands of CO-OP tea through to testing them on parents and even on real customers in their stores) with year 6. Stoughton Infant School has its children growing plants, harvesting the seeds then packaging them to sell back to the parents. They love it. The children at that school believe they can do anything. They are given responsibilities and allowed to take appropriate risks.

Most of our successful business leaders are men. I suggest that these entrepreneurs have taken several risks in their lives.

I believe that many of our children today are closeted. Parents are concerned at the risks in Western society today and frequently over-protect their children.

We need to take action through PACCT (Chapter 11) to make our communities not only safer but also welcoming to children. We need to find ways for parents to trust boys in the community and trust our community to look out for them. In Holland there are fabulous schemes where streets become Home Zones. Boys and girls play out together, gaining first-hand experience of risk and responsibility in our real world rather than the virtual one so many of our boys inhabit.

How would the world progress without risk takers? Would we have ever walked on the moon? Would we have submarines or antibiotics? So many successes in our society are down to risks being taken, the majority of these by men. The resulting successes go on to inspire the next generation of risk takers, boys and girls alike, who in turn inspire future generations. Risk taking, in the right context is good.

I believe all schools should have a 'Risk and Responsibility Policy' (Chapter 11) that they agree with the children and parents. This will help us all, especially next winter when the boys are desperate to throw snowballs or in the autumn and the contentious activity of playing conkers comes round again. Schools should set up specific activities and areas where risk taking within agreed bounds is permitted; children might even be allowed to break out of the cotton wool cocoon and be children again!

Points for Action – Bigger and Better

Boys are reluctant to ask for help. Remember this in school and at home. 'Would you like me to show you that again' is gentler on the self-esteem than 'Who needs more help' or having to put hands up in class.

Praise much more than you criticize. Always look 'beyond the behaviour' but if criticism is necessary be sure it is quiet, calm and respectful.

Be sure all teaching, but especially setting and streaming, offers open-ended activities and investigations with real purpose.

Initiate a risk and responsibility policy in your school.

Investigate 'Home Zones' and creative ways to make our communities safer for boys.

The big outdoors

Making things

Boys are often good at construction, making dens and shelters as well as house construction as adults. Dads and lads together are happiest when doing outdoor stuff especially when it involves building or making something. This often involves mathematical and scientific skills as well as good three-dimensional and spatial awareness. A group called 'Who let the Dads out!' for all dads, but especially those with Saturday access only, has been set up in Surrey. They get together once a month to do practical tasks with their kids.

One of the most successful has been designing, building and of course racing go-karts. In order to get boys and their dads involved a practical task and purpose (Chapter 11) is one of the best ways in.

Tools and weapons

Boys continually collect sticks and stones, sometimes to make things, sometimes just because they can. In order to build things boys and men need tools. It is as if they know this from a very young age. They love sharp stones or strong rocks, sticks that can be made into something, a catapult, a hammer, often a pretend gun. One childminder told me of a gentle boy she minds who loves rich tea finger biscuits, not because of the taste . . . he nibbles each biscuit and makes it into a gun! We can keep our schools and nurseries free of toy guns but some boys will find ways whatever equipment they have.

We need to give boys opportunities to learn to use and respect proper tools with appropriate guidance. Their results are so much better and the experiences more relevant when real tools are available.

Things that move

Have you ever wondered why boys are so keen on playing with cars, bikes etc.? They are fascinated by how things work, levers, pulleys, engines. They love bikes and go-karts and modifying any vehicle to make it go faster or be stronger. Scientific and mathematical angles into subjects often work really well for boys. Windham Nursery School has a video player and screwdrivers for children to dismantle. Although this is not transport, boys love to see how anything works. They love gadgets and this is one reason new technology appeals so much to males – they want to know how things work. Hands-on practical approaches such as dismantling a bike or a bit of an engine work brilliantly for boys. My neighbour is forever fixing cars and he is like a magnetic attraction for my boys and such a good mentor and role model. Transport and things that move seems to be a passion from the cradle to the grave.

Projects with a purpose

Barnett Wood Infants gets its parents involved from the word go. It gives each new set of reception class parents a specific project to achieve, usually in the school grounds. This has the fantastic effect of getting parents, especially dads working together for a common purpose, bringing in expertize and finance, often from local businesses and building something fabulous for the school in the process. Very often the children get involved too helping with the design and build. They then are much more likely to take care of the new apparatus as they appreciate all the effort that people they care about have put in. Of course with dads involved this has to be the biggest and best project yet. Confident boys, at any age, are very good at thinking big.

Long term, the project also means that this class of parents know and support each other and their children, feel happy and welcome at the school. They build a community support network without even knowing it. SAGE (Chapter 11), a similar project, can be used with groups of boys from seven plus, helping them to take responsibility and work together towards a shared passion and purpose focused around something else boys are good at . . . eating!

Points for Action – The Big Outdoors

Get dads and boys involved in school together (especially on Saturdays) using practical activities based on what boys are good at. (Remember to make things fair for mums and girls too!)

Give boys opportunities to learn to use real tools safely, especially if they have a role model to help them.

Invite groups of new parents to take on a specific project as they join the school.

Transport is a real focus for boys. Use this to set up workshops to help them learn to fix bikes, make go-karts or design rafts with good role models from the community.

Think outside the box – how can you use food to get dads, mums and members of the community involved in schools.

Being focused

Single-minded or spontaneous and impulsive?

Boys are good at being spontaneous and impulsive; they can flit from one task to the next if they think the next thing might be better. If you have any doubts about this observe a boy in a nursery setting or an adult male with the TV remote. This is fine until they find something they have got the right skills for, they enjoy and have a purpose. When these conditions are in place then boys are single-minded. Try asking a boy a question when he is absorbed in building a model or watching his favourite team. He can barely hear you (Chapter 7). The ability to focus on one task to the exclusion of all around you is a valuable skill, certainly one that I would benefit from at times as a typical multi-tasking female. Boys are also good at arguing, standing up for the things they believe in and challenging things that may get in the way of this.

Teachers and parents need to appreciate this focus, this single-mindedness in schools and at home. We need to give boys many more opportunities to do one thing at once for a sustained period other than those where they are glued to a screen. Beware! This 'thing' must have a real purpose for that boy. We need to know this boy, to help him find his purpose.

Back at Ripley Infants, a class of seven-year-olds was asked to design and build the lighthouse from the story 'The Lighthouse Keeper's Lunch' by Ronda and David Armitage. The teacher did not plan overtly to be 'boy-friendly' in her approach but so many things in that session built in success for the boys.

They were allowed to let the task run over several sessions; they did not have to do it in bite-sized chunks. (Small clear steps in instructions are really useful but being torn away from an activity they are truly engaged in is frustrating for so many boys.)

The boys had torn, cut and made quite a mess on the floor. At no point were they reprimanded for being untidy; they were allowed to continue in the way that worked best for them. They were so focused on the construction that the peripherals of picking up the paper just went unseen. (Organization and tidiness are valuable skills but not part of the success criteria for this task and can get in the way.) When I learned to be tolerant to this style of learning and the reasons behind it, life in my boy-heavy household became so much calmer.

Although some theories say that children have one minute of attention span per year of age, others say that the attention span of most boys is only ever four minutes. I'm not sure who has sat and counted or how this caters for the differences between each child. I do believe, however, that boys have a short attention span for things they have not initiated and we need to take this into consideration in long sessions wherever they are.

The flip side is, if a boy is allowed to follow his passion he can focus on a chosen activity for extended periods. Why do we battle to ring the changes every few minutes to get the boys and girls to stick to our agenda? Sometimes it is necessary but why not try, let them follow their skills, learn through play and investigation, for at least some of the time. I firmly believe life will be happier and more productive for all concerned.

'Screen suction'

Boys are typically good at focusing on screens. It literally draws them in and keeps them absorbed. It is connected with being absorbed in one thing at once but is also linked to the fact that boys are much more visually oriented. Images rather than words fuel the way most boys process information. Surely images are what screens do best. Screens are positioned where boys are geared to look, they are geared to look straight ahead, one reason they are so good at activities involving targets. Figuratively speaking, boys can zoom in their vision like a digital camera. They can focus on the object of their attention and literally not see other things around. It is almost like they see the Satellite Navigation screen and not the view out of the windows.

Consider this . . . A young man was with me on an activity holiday and we were walking to the archery. I was ahead and, passing a towel that had fallen off a railing, I stopped to pick it up. There was a second towel on the ground and I deliberately left it to see if my example would be followed. The young man in question walked right past it. When I asked him, 'Why didn't you pick up that towel?' he replied . . .

'What towel?'

He had simply not seen it. His focus was unashamedly on what he was about to do.

How much conflict and misunderstanding could be avoided in male–female relationships both in homes and schools if we all understood a little better how males and females view the world differently (Brain Wiring).

Just say it

Boys are good at saying only the words that are needed. This is often frustrating for the women in their lives who need to use so many more words each day. It is hardly surprising that there are arguments if you follow the work of Allan and Barbara Pease who suggest that, including vocal sounds and body language gestures, men use around 7,000 'words' a day whereas women use around 18,000. This has huge implications in the classroom.

Women teachers and teaching assistants, especially those supporting boys with special needs, often use many words, intending to be kind and supportive.

'Hello there, when you have finished that puzzle, oh haven't you done well, you've nearly finished the whole of the tractor, please put all the pieces back into the box, put the lid on carefully and put the puzzle back onto the shelf. Do you know where it goes? Yes the blue shelf, next to the building blocks. There's a good lad. Then come and sit on the carpet. Thank you.'

How likely is it that Luke will do as he is asked? He probably has already forgotten the initial task. He has received far too many instructions and is most likely to be, at best confused, at worst, completely switched off.

Luke is much more likely to do as he is asked if the instruction is clear, concise, has eye contact and mentions his name.

'Luke, eyes please, put the puzzle away. Thanks'.

The result . . . less noise, less distraction, less frustration, better behaviour, better relationships.

There are also implications for parents using too many words with boys at home or falling into the trap of asking for things to be done several times. If we ask a boy of any age to do a task and we ask ten or more times, how is he to know which time is the last, which time is the one that is really supposed to mean it. How do you know it is the last time of asking unless you wait to hear if it is asked again. I am fascinated by the subject of different styles of communication between males and females and how a few little changes can make such a difference to lives and relationships at home or at school.

As well as women being aware of how many words they are likely to speak it is important that boys know that their responses can often seem too brief or the instructions of male teachers too succinct, even curt for the girls they are teaching.

The skill most males have of being succinct comes through when they are doing a science experiment. They have a visual picture of what they want to do and know what they need. They often see little point in recording wordy accounts and find this frustrating.

Just like the excessive use of grids and frameworks to help boys plan their stories we need to be sure that boys are also allowed many opportunities to 'just go for it' in the way that suits them and their preferred learning style (Chapter 7).

Boys are also good at doing the one thing they are focused on without finding the need to do other jobs around them. Girls are more likely to line up the scissors in their box tidily before taking a pair to cut with. Boys will just grab the scissors and get on with their cutting.

As boys move into adulthood they are often much more efficient than women in meetings. Meeting led by men are typically much more sharp, focused and frequently shorter than those by women. This efficiency and skill of 'cutting to the quick' may well contribute to the fact that many business leaders are men. A great number of them are strongly dominant in the skills of the right brain and a surprising number are either dyslexic or have characteristics in line with ADHD – both typically associated with a dominant right hemisphere (Chapter 7).

We need to recognize these leadership skills in boys, focus them and help them direct them positively. Alongside this we need to help boys develop the skills that come less easily . . . social skills are often an area where the brightest boys struggle. Each and every boy is different. We, as the adults who care for boys, have the privilege and responsibility to believe in them and the opportunity to get it right for the future.

Points for Action – Being Focused

Be patient and understanding when boys don't see things outside their main 'target focus'.

Allow boys more opportunities at school and at home to focus on one purposeful activity where they can experience success.

Resist insisting that boys work tidily or record every stage if this interrupts their creativity and focus (within safe and reasonable limits).

Avoid lengthy spells of expecting boys to listen and remain focused. Remember boys generally learn visually and need fewer words than girls.

Understand and accommodate the fact that males and females view the world differently.

Big issues for boys

'Britain's children are the unhappiest children in the West, according to a 2007 UNICEF study of 21 industrialised countries.'

'Not only do they drink the most, smoke more and have more sex than their peers, they rate their health as the poorest, dislike school more and are among the least satisfied with life.'

This quote from *The Times* tells us nothing new. For several years we have been made aware, all too eagerly, by much of the media, of how bad life is for children and how poorly children behave and achieve, especially the boys. The reason this UNICEF report made us take stock is because it shows us in stark contrast with other Western cultures.

It seems that, not only do we mistrust men but we no longer trust our instincts. We lack faith in the judgements of parents and education professionals. We often lack faith in our own judgements. Only if facts are matched with evidence and numbers, when we know where we lie in the league tables, do we sit up and take notice, and it goes further than the specifics in the report. Sue Palmer, in her recent book, describes our young people's lives as 'Toxic Childhood'. It is truly shocking but perhaps a stark awakening is what is needed in order to begin to make things better.

Children are educated at school but they learn every minute of their waking day. We have some control over what goes on in our communities, our families but less control over the influences of society including technology and the media.

> Children are educated at school but they learn every minute of their waking day.

The twenty-first century is raising challenges for families and for bringing up children in Western society in a way that we have not seen since the industrial revolution. We have become blasé if not blinkered to so many aspects of the way we treat children, especially boys, in Western society today.

I wonder how many people in the Victorian times knew it was wrong to send children up chimneys or to use them as child labour but because they were only one person and so many people were following the pattern they felt powerless to resist.

We can begin by looking at the individual child and how best we can understand him, what he needs and how we can make that happen. By the time you have finished this book you will have so many simple solutions at your fingertips you will feel empowered, you will feel brave to fight for the future of boys and men, you alone will make a difference but get together with like-minded others and your ripples will make real changes to the lives of real children, to the lives of real boys.

Money and work

In family life today what would you consider to be indicators of success? Would it be confident, contented children, calm, happy families with time to be able to enjoy life together or would it be a generous income, smart cars, foreign holidays and the latest technology?

It is very difficult with external pressures to be confident with what you have, to step back from working long hours or buying the latest car. If you are on a low income it is very difficult to see the things that so many others have and not want them for your own family. This is how so many get into such horrendous debt so easily.

> Some children go to so many activities after school and in the holidays that they are figuratively 'clubbed to death'.

We live in a NOW culture. Children in all social strata are well aware of what possessions they could have and want them NOW. Parents on low income feel guilty that their children are going without. Working parents feel guilty about the lack of time they have with their children and so buy them more and more material possessions or pay for expensive childcare, hobbies and clubs. Some children go to so many activities after school and in the holidays that they are figuratively 'clubbed to death'. Many children have so many toys that they are spoiled for choice. Those that have little choice usually have television or computer games and spend much of their time, especially boys pulled in by 'Screen Suction'. Adults too have screens as their default relaxation. Boys' screens make decisions for them, they become their parents and family, their computer games take over from friendships and learning through play. Boys rarely find time to relax without a screen or a phone, to make their own constructive entertainment or just BE with friends. No wonder young people struggle when given freedom in their teenage years. They simply do not have the skills for the real world.

Many parents, overworked or unemployed, are so stressed when they are at home that the time they have with their children leads to less-than-healthy relationships. Many women have such low opinions of men and readily pass these on to others including their own sons. In a large number of families children do not see their fathers from one day to the next and many fathers are missing from everyday families completely.

There are similar challenges in schools with budgets tight and around thirty pupils per class, teachers often have less time, energy or patience than would enable them to do the job as thoroughly as they would choose. Every child deserves the very best experience in school yet I wonder if all teachers are truly in a position to be able to offer this?

The media shows all children the new things they could have. They would prefer a new one rather than learning thrifty skills from their parents such as repairing, fixing, mending, making. It is often far easier to replace than repair.

We are preparing children for a life where they will always expect to have access to money and possessions. What will happen if, more realistically, these children are short of money at any time in their life? They will struggle to make ends meet; they will lack the skills to solve their own problems; they will not know the value of helping others and asking for help themselves.

Children are used to having things NOW. Even teachers are seeing that twenty-first century children are more demanding. They have pretty much all they need available on demand. The concept of saving up for a new bike seems to be a thing of the past, so are we surprised that the level of debt in Britain is so alarming.

Higher levels of qualifications are needed for even the simplest of jobs and when the competition for these is too tough, what happens to those who haven't made the grade? They even have a name . . . NEETs (Not in Education Employment or Training). They frequently turn to drugs and alcohol followed by crime to pay for these. Cheap imports and new technology make apprenticeships and manual, artisan jobs harder to come by and new immigrant workers make these harder still to find.

The skills needed in business today are those softer skills, people skills and communication skills for the service industries. These skills are more easily found in females making it harder still for young males to get their first job.

The assets of business are no longer in stock or products but in the quality of the people who work for them. Good relationships and social skills alongside a broad, high-quality education accessible to all are key to the future of our young people. How does a life in front of a screen with few social interactions prepare our boys for this future?

> The assets of business are no longer in stock or products but in the quality of the people who work for them.

When young people go on to university they are immediately saddled with debt establishing a pattern that becomes part of everyday life. They begin their adult life 'treading water' financially and find the only way to move forward is through more loans and credit cards. Where does the cycle end? Just recently the Brown government in Britain has announced that there will be lessons in managing finance and debt as part of secondary education. Quite a contrast to the 1970s when children were encouraged to buy savings stamps at school!

So we have a consumer society, yet there is more and more debt. People still want material possessions even if they do not have the means to buy them. Debt becomes worse and many families are in poverty.

'We are heading for a serious social crisis. And this poses a huge challenge for our children. They are the adults of the future it will effect every strand of their lives. It is paramount for their future that something changes and it changes fast' (Poverty and wealth across Britain 1968 to 2005, July 2007).

> 'Every index – income, property, health and longevity, educational and occupational achievement – reveals a less equal society than at any other point in modern times' (Feel-Bad Britain; A View from the Democratic Left).

It seems like we are living in a society of extremes with this underlying so many of the conflicts that cause challenges to families, children and communities. Affluent or not, children today struggle to entertain themselves without it costing a fortune. There are so many cinemas, theme parks, computer games and fast food diners that families trying to stick to a budget are under pressure to entertain their children by throwing yet more money at them. No one is denying that having a reasonable income is an important factor in family life. No child should have to live in poverty yet all children need to have times without money to burn. They need to be drawn away from technology to learn to play, to learn to socialize with other children. They need to find ways of having fun for free ... playing in the park, playing in the garden, drawing, imagining, playing with other children, getting wet and dirty, making things from junk ... the list goes on.

So much of people's lives today is fuelled by money, the need to earn it or doing things that cost money that then fuel the need to work even harder. I call this the 'Gold rush'. Are we too busy rushing every aspect in our lives to 'get the gold' that we have no time to stop and see the wealth we already have, the pure health, the simple wealth, the few necessary possessions and more importantly the precious people, the children, the families, the schools, the boys?

Time and space

Why is it that there never seems to be enough time these days? However long we have there always seem to be too many things to fit in. Life is complex. There are always more jobs to do than there are hours in the day. We have so many time-saving devices in modern life yet, as parents or education professionals, the stresses of time are eating away at the *human* aspects of our lives.

We live in a high speed, instant culture, you might say a microwave culture, one where we look out for ourselves, cook fast, eat fast and move on fast. Where in all this rush does time for people appear? In society as a whole there seems to be a distinct lack of time for ourselves and for others.

Unless we have time to really build a relationship with the children we teach, care for or parent, we cannot really know how best to help them grow and succeed.

Children are pressured to do too much too soon, to grow up too quickly. They know about so many things through worldwide media. They have tried so many things and had so many experiences by the time they are teenagers that they look for new excitement. They frequently turn to drugs, alcohol and sex. On the surface they appear to have grown up but beneath the bravado on the exterior they are still immature children in many ways. Their factory-farmed childhoods have meant that, boys particularly, have been so busy with study and tests, screens or prescribed activities that they are still immature in communication, organization, independent thought, socialization. They lack the skills to solve their own problems, to occupy their time without screens and most alarming to sustain relationships. They appear to have grown up fast but when it comes to commitment and skills for relating to others, especially when the going is tough, some are gravely lacking, many are angry, defensive and aggressive. Many are scared.

In order to have relationships we *have to* communicate. Even communication has become a high-speed activity. We text, e-mail and flit from one thing to another so quickly on the internet that it has destroyed much of our face-to-face communication. Mobile phones dominate everywhere. Electronic communication certainly is a valuable tool yet it causes stress and can seriously damage relationships.

Another thing we forget about people and especially children is that they are fallible, unpredictable and needy. Somewhere in our busy lives we need to plan in some slack for those times when things do not run according to plan, when someone is ill or simply needs a little extra help or support. We need to plan in time for people together and for people alone.

There is always technology . . . TV, computers, play stations, even mums using mobile phones as they walk their children to the park. Technology has taken over our lives. It is always there, ready to use. It is already created and meets our needs with minimum effort from us. It is so simple to switch on a TV or computer as a default. It moves so quickly and rarely challenges us outside our comfort zone. Technology is the first thing we turn to in everything we do. We need to teach our children to discriminate and not to binge on technology because it is there and it is easy to access.

Society no longer knows how to do *nothing*.

Children find it hard to be creative and entertain themselves. Children never get the opportunity to 'be'. They have little or no tolerance for stillness, moving at a slower pace or being bored. These aspects of life are vital if we are to be creative and inventive. So much is already discovered and there on a plate for all that children have a lack of purpose and drive. They have a less apparent need to create things for themselves and be inventive. We are losing these skills!

For some time I had admired the skills of a particular colleague. He was a busy man with many roles and demands in his successful working life. He had five happy children and a thriving marriage. He was building an extension on his house yet was calm, never appeared stressed and always had time and space for people. How did he do it? His answer was simple. He only ever scheduled his diary to 70 per cent.

When I first discovered this I was taken aback. Surely 70 per cent would be seen as slack or lazy. In the Western culture of long hours and being seen to be

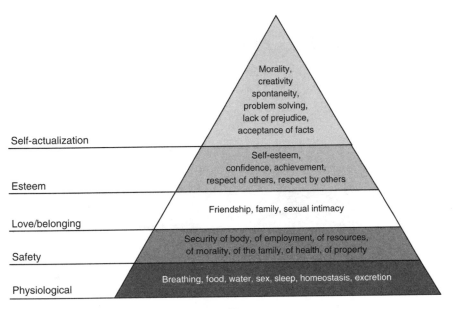

Maslow's hierarchy.

the last one out of the office this would be frowned upon. It surely couldn't work. However as I thought more and more about it I realized why it did work.

We are much more efficient when we have had time to think, when our bodies are healthy and when our personal needs are met (see fig 3.1 Maslow's hierarchy).

Teachers or parents, we are at our least efficient when we are stressed, tired, ill, worried, all things which are more likely when we miss lunch, have no time for boys, for those we love let alone time for ourselves.

In this context, how do working parents and teachers balance out the high demands and long hours with having time to be there and be human for their children whether their own or those in their class?

Parents juggle their commitments and prioritize their lives in a variety of ways. I suggest there are three types of parents: 'floor', 'sofa' and 'pedestal' parents.

The floor parents prioritize time with their child. They are often there where the child is, on the floor playing with the farm or helping to build the model for school homework. They join in with what their child is doing and talk as they play together.

The sofa parents are sitting on the sofa (hopefully awake) and occasionally commenting on what their child is doing on the floor. They have made time to be with their child but they are alongside the action rather than taking an

active part. They may be talking to their child but equally well they may be reading, working on their laptop or watching their favourite soap opera.

The third type of parents are the pedestal parents. They may well be absent through work commitments, through family breakdown or other circumstances. There may be a picture of those parents placed on a pedestal or the parents may be there in body but so tired and stressed that they may as well be on a pedestal. 'Leave your father alone he's had a tough day!'

As a nation, I believe that whether or not we are parents there are more pedestal type relationships between adults and children than floor type ones.

Western society seems to have little time and space for children.

'Those who observe us from abroad believe much of our problem (with children) lies in the peculiar harshness with which we in this country view childhood in general' (*Sunday Times Magazine*, 18 March 2007).

People holidaying in Britain have complained that holiday resorts are not as child-friendly and welcoming as many abroad. In Britain people seem to be so worried about what others will think of children and their behaviour that parents tell them off, pretend they are not there and get stressed in situations where a 'firm, calm approach' (Palmer) would work much better. Adults and children in Britain need to stop avoiding each other and learn how to *BE* together.

British society in crisis is a burning issue right now with David Cameron, leader of the Conservative Party talking about a 'pro-social society' in his speech to the Centre for Social Justice in July 2007. This top-down approach can only help, but society is about people first and foremost and in order to change, *individuals* have to be empowered.

We have the power in schools and families to prioritize, to find time and space for boys, for children, for adults. *We* need to make time and space for these changes in society from the grass roots up. The future begins with us.

Responsibility and relationships

In the Western world we live in a disposable culture. Are we aware that we have now begun applying this culture to our relationships? If the going gets tough we have few role models of persistence and ways to overcome difficulties that it seems to be easier to give up relationships and start a new one. We relinquish responsibility.

Although sustaining a damaging relationship is certainly unwise, so many families break down over issues that could be overcome with time, effort and support. So few parents find time to nurture the relationship between each other or to enjoy a shared hobby or passion.

How are boys supposed to learn how to be good fathers if so many live without a father figure to relate to?

Fragmented families cause our twenty-first-century children to feel insecure, cause huge difficulties for the adults in those families and can lead to stress, illness, conflict and real health issues for parents and children. To solve problems whether adult to adult, adult to child or child to child takes time. Time to care about solving problems takes a relationship between the parties involved, and this takes time on a regular basis, at home, in communities or at school.

In British schools exclusion is one of the strategies we use far too frequently to cope with challenging behaviour. The majority of these excluded children are boys.

In Britain we use exclusion more than ever.
'Permanent exclusions from school are growing. They have increased fourfold from 2,910 in 1990/1 to 12,476 in 1995/6, the latest year for which data is available' (New Policy Institute Second Chances Exclusion From School).

We need systems in place to support schools, to allow them time and space to help them take greater responsibility from within to maintain relationships with boys and their parents to build positive futures for these young people.

There are close links between school exclusions and crime as young adults. If we are to live in a healthy society with healthy young people we *must* take responsibility as individuals, as a society, finding creative ways to be more proactive to support boys, not 'dispose of them'.

In schools we schedule in literacy and numeracy hours in schools, time for preparing for tests. In families we schedule in martial arts or swimming lessons, East Enders or Neighbours but without it formally on the timetable do we remember to schedule in time each day for relationships, for people?

With only a token investment of time people have only token relationships. As boys are generally less forthcoming with conversation than girls, it follows that it takes a deliberate effort to spend time and develop a trusting relationship with a boy.

It is relationships that enable us to know the person we are with, whether that is a toddler, a teenager, a colleague or an elderly person in our neighbourhood.

We can easily lack respect for the people and environment around us because we know so little about them. Without respect it is so difficult to see the need for each and every one of us to take responsibility.

If there is a problem and we do nothing perhaps someone else will tackle it. Children and also adults frequently sidestep challenges, ignoring them and seeming not to care.

We live in a selfish culture and in order to break that we need to care, to take responsibility as individuals and as a society, to respect our physical environment, our fellow human beings and most importantly ourselves. This is the message we need to get over loud and clear to all our young people today with words but more powerfully with our actions.

Our world is not disposable, nor are the young people in it. Each of us must take responsibility and we must take it now!

Fear and blame

Would you intervene if a teenager was causing damage to property?

Very few people would. They may call the police but they would be unlikely to step in or even speak to that teenager. Would this be different if the young person was nine years old or even five?

Why is it that so many adults feel disempowered to step in and take control in the Western world today? The simple answer is fear.

They are scared that they may get hurt; they are scared that in trying to help they may be blamed, be accused of an offence themselves. Unless they know the youngster's name even teachers are unlikely to intervene out of school.

It is as if each of us live in a bubble. Children are unlikely to look inside their own little bubble to take responsibility or to find a solution when there is a problem; they are more likely to look beyond their own bubble to what someone else did or didn't do. Young people know their rights but struggle hugely with responsibilities.

Society and the media judge and condemn struggling schools. Teachers are so afraid of doing badly in Ofsted inspections or having low test results that in many schools jumping through the hoops to achieve the best results has taken over from the most important focus, the individuals, the children, the passion. Schools and parents alike are forever being told what to do from the top down. Everything has to be recorded in triplicate in case professionals are sued. Everything has to be risk assessed and the children are figuratively wrapped in cotton wool. At last, the Secretary of State for Children Schools and Families, Ed Balls has launched a consultation on how to maintain a balance between keeping children safe and helping them to learn how to handle risk. Life is bound with so many rules that people have forgotten how to be creative, inventive, to relax a little and enjoy learning, teaching, life and each other.

In Britain we are very quick to see what is bad, what is wrong. 'There is something deep in our culture that leads to a belief that we should be punitive towards children who are difficult' (David Jones International Federation of Social Workers, *Sunday Times*, 18 March 2007).

Despite the 'Children are Unbeatable Alliance' (DFES) and the best efforts of Parenting UK, Britain is one of very few countries in the European State still to allow corporal punishment of children. Many adults are loathe to give up the right to smack as they struggle with alternative ways of overcoming challenging behaviour. Physical punishment in itself is based on fear. It is vital for our future to develop relationships based on respect.

In contrast to physical punishment, many adults are petrified of offering appropriate physical comfort to a distressed child. Boys in particular are still discouraged from crying and encouraged to practice the British 'stiff upper lip'.

We need to get to know each child and his many strands and strengths. Rather than our first response being ABC:

- anger
- blame
- condemnation

This is a particularly big issue for boys as their natural outgoing physical behaviours are more apparent and often more criticized than the natural behaviours of girls (Chapter 5).

Children in our society are more likely to be noticed, ostracized and criticized for 'bad' behaviour than noticed, cuddled and praised for 'good' behaviour. Many young boys are treated as if they are already men, frequently with the disdain, anger and venom so often aimed at adult males by women who have had negative experiences with the men in their lives.

Parents are expected to be able to cope and feel it reflects back to them if their children are in trouble. They are often worried about what other people will think of them. Seeming to be in charge and controlling, especially of boys, helps them to feel they are keeping their social respect even if their child's self-esteem and confidence fall foul in the process.

Many parents have a lack of trust of the very agencies that could help them, and still considerable numbers are fearful of getting involved in schools. This has to change. Schools must find ways of involving all parents, not just those who give so willingly of their time and commitment. All parents need to feel welcomed and valued.

> Schools are the lynch pin for helping children stay safe and avoiding getting into trouble.

Again our punitive culture condemns our children far too quickly. In Britain we criminalize at ten, the lowest age in Europe. In most other countries the age of criminalization is fourteen. Once labelled and in the punitive system it is very hard to break out of that pattern. If young men re-offend and are given a custodial sentence a negative spiral is triggered. What has begun in childhood, in childish behaviours goes on to taint their adult lives.

'More than three quarters of 18-20 year olds are reconvicted after leaving prison' (Barrow Cadbury Trust).

Just consider how many prisons in Britain are for males and how many for females. Our boys have good reason to be fearful of their future.

The punitive culture has become even worse since police have been given targets to clear up crime.

'Children are being arrested for throwing cream buns and bits of cucumber!' (Stuart Tendler, *The Times*, 15 May 2007). This does begin to seem ridiculous. How else do we treat boys that will seem ridiculous in years to come?

Young people feel backed into a corner; they feel scared and often this comes out through anger and aggression, fear and blame. This is again reprimanded and the downward spiral continues. It is imperative that we break this pattern and reverse the downward spiral of society in order to build a positive future for everyone.

Changing roles and expectations

Throughout the early twentieth century expectations of men and women had been quite clearly defined. It was expected that most women stay at home and look after families. Men were seen as the breadwinners and went out to work. During the Second World War many women became empowered in areas not previously deemed to be in a woman's domain. They may have worked on the land and in factories but the biggest change was that they learned to do many things without men. Attitudes towards men began to change!

Schooling throughout the war years had taken a low priority but there was soon to be greater access to education for girls and boys. Girls were becoming much better educated and able to take more control over their lives especially with the advent of the contraceptive pill in the 1960s.

In 1975 the Sex Discrimination Act came into force.

'The duty gives public authorities legal responsibility for demonstrating that they treat women and men fairly.'

This had a huge effect as women were now expected to be treated as equals. Although this act was designed to promote equality across the genders it actually worked much more heavily in favour of women as, up to that time they had been treated far from equally.

The impact of this in schools swung the pendulum to the extreme and extremes are never good. What happened for boys was that they had to be offered the very same opportunities as girls and vice versa. Being treated fairly is of course important but does being treated fairly and being treated equally amount to the same thing?

Sadly in all of the equality, many of the good practices in educating boys got swept away with the bad. By the beginning of the 1980s when I first qualified, teachers were no longer allowed to consider that boys and girls had any differences in their needs whatsoever.

Things changed in schools and they changed in homes. Women were emancipated and men were now expected to take more active roles with the house and family. They were expected to change nappies, cook, clean, shop, in fact frequently take equal shares in the running of the home. This coincided with the 'Every man for himself' cut and thrust attitude in businesses in the 1980s. Jobs were no longer for life and with the boom in house prices men were expected to provide financially, gain promotion with bigger cars and materialistic trappings while playing a greater part in home life. More and more women were going out to work and roles overlapped resulting in family life and relationships, physical and emotional well-being falling dangerously low in the list of priorities. The pressures were all too much and the valve that blew first was that of the family. Divorce rates rocketed and fragmented families became the norm.

People moved around the country more to seek jobs and opportunities. Grandparents and cousins were no longer round the corner to give advice, share a meal or help to look after the children. People spent longer each day travelling to jobs having less time to spend in the local communities. Communities began to crumble. Life got harder for stay-at-home parents as well as for those juggling jobs and children. Is it surprising then that a generation of toddlers were parked in front of the TV to give these fraught parents a break? The situation does not look good.

As technology advanced, this changed the face of so many businesses. Factory jobs could be done more easily by robots and the range of work available narrowed considerably. Apprenticeships were no longer readily available and cheap labour abroad moved many jobs away from our shores. The need for higher levels of education to compete for the remaining jobs became acute. Unless well educated it became increasingly harder for boys to get jobs. Those that had jobs felt pressured to work longer hours to prove their worth and so the children lost out on their fathers (and often mothers) yet again.

During the 1980s people had become more selfish, more insular and the culture for blame turned into an explosion of suing. People became fearful that if they did anything wrong they would get sued so they had policies for everything, checklists for work and school. People stopped being impulsive and vibrant and became defensive and worried. On the positive side corporal punishment was stopped in school but this led to many adults feeling powerless and children feeling empowered. People working with children stopped taking risks and began taking out personal liability insurance.

Children too joined in the blame culture. We swung from children being seen and not heard in the 1950s where any child's accusation against an adult was quashed or beaten out of them to children being believed above adults. Good teachers, good youth leaders left their professions for fear that they would be accused by a child and condemned as a paedophile.

All children but especially boys lost out as the good men in their lives gradually disappeared; raising boys was not a priority. Now in the noughties we are paying the price and we have to redress the balance. The recent introduction of the Gender Equality Duty begins to accept that there are differences between men and women, that boys and girls may have different needs, different learning styles. Now we have a licence to 'Make It Better for Boys' in order to change the face of our future.

4 Media and labelling – the power of stereotypes

The male–female continuum

Take a rope . . . Stretch the rope out into a straight line. Now imagine that at one end there is a life-sized model of a man, a man you know only from the media. He needs to be portrayed as strong, muscled, aggressive; in fact he needs to have characteristics that are seen as being *stereotypically* male. Perhaps Arnold Schwarzenegger?

I have no way of knowing what Arnie is like in real life. All I know of him is what I have seen, heard or read . . . judgements made and messages passed on by other people. He may in reality have traits that are far from the stereotypical view of males but as I do not know him personally I am not familiar with these.

At the other end of the rope imagine a life-sized model of a female. She needs to be delicate, pretty, beautifully dressed, in fact stereotypically female. Perhaps Keira Knightley could match this brief? Again, without knowing her personally it is impossible to know if she has less-than-typical traits in real life but the media view comes over to me as feminine through and through.

The rope now becomes a continuum between the extremes of thoroughly masculine and thoroughly feminine. If you were to unravel the rope you would find it is made up of many strands, not just a single line. It reflects the complex make-up of each one of us. However, is being masculine and feminine, typically male or female a simplistic black and white judgement? We are in danger of jumping to conclusions about complex personalities based on these extremes but just like the rope in our continuum, every person on earth is made up of a complex weave, weathered and worn by its journey in life.

Consider, if you were to place yourself on that rope continuum, where would you be? At one end or somewhere in the middle? Would this be the same for all strands of your personality or do you have some strands that better match the perceived view of the opposite gender, the one so frequently

portrayed by the media? Would your position on this continuum be the same tomorrow or do your characteristics and behaviour change according to mood, who you are with or the time of the day?

Now consider how often we hear people making comments about males based on stereotypical preconceptions. 'That's just like a boy', 'That's men for you', 'Boys will be boys!' and frequently 'just like his father' in a less than complementary tone of voice.

This negative view of males as a species is perpetuated by the media on a daily basis.

Media

This negative view of males as a species is perpetuated by the media on a daily basis.

In a world where boys have fewer and fewer good male role models active in their lives they are magnetically drawn to the role model feted by the media . . . footballers assaulting each other, drunken celebrities behaving badly, sportsmen taking drugs, lager louts giving the British a bad reputation on the 'Costas', politicians lying, absent fathers, hoodies, gangs, drugs, vandalism, paedophilia, mugging, rape, road rage, foul language . . . the list goes on. Even quiz shows are based on rejecting the least popular, insulting people and condemning 'the weakest link'.

The newspapers are worse in many ways with powerful advertising alongside the attention-grabbing headlines and the repeated attention drawn to how badly our boys behave and perform in school used as a political tool. Boys are pawns in a media game and from my viewpoint they always lose!

The news is unavoidable but the British culture is much like the news. We are always quick to spot what is going wrong, to complain rather than complement. It seems to be unacceptable to have pride in what we do well, what is good. Children's news programmes really need to be aware of the important balance it needs to project. It needs to ensure that what young people see is not all doom and gloom; all boys are not bad. We already live in fearful communities. If we continually focus on the bad things we will see more and more. 'What you pay attention to is what you get more of' (Hunt).

Programming has a lot to answer for. In every house-building, moving abroad, or achieving a project type of programme there are always negative, pessimistic projections of what could go wrong next leaving us on a down before the next section or the advert break. Is this how the world is encouraged to view life?

Dedicated children's television is even worse. It has been a painful process for me, in the name of research, to sit through some of the horrendous programmes churned out endlessly to be brainwashed into believing that: Boys are stupid, lazy, aggressive, sulky, violent and rude.

This is perpetuated by the merchandizing that is unavoidable. Today's toy shops would be all but empty if the products linked to TV programmes and movies were to be removed.

Clothing carries media images too and boys want to wear tough guy T-shirts to be like their favourite role model whether or not that role model is a positive one. Have you noticed that the role models and characters aimed at young boys change, from warm, caring, community-spirited folk such as Fireman Sam and Postman Pat to Power Rangers, Ninja Turtles and other fighting males at around the age of four (Chapter 6) ? Research at the Centre for Child Mental Health shows how powerful the influence of behaviour on television is to young children. Why do we give aggressive role models at the age our boys are expected to socialize, be calm and compliant . . . when they begin school? Perhaps even worse, the men, the role models in children's programmes, are ridiculed, ignored, jeered at, disrespected or are portrayed as evil through and through.

Children watch on an average three hours' television a day, boys more than girls (Media Smart).
'. . . with the strong messages it sends out to our young people is it any wonder that every school day in 2006 over 200 pupils under 11 were sent home for bad behaviour ?' (Julie Greenhough, *Times Educational Supplement*, 18 May 2007).

'If we accept, as we must, that the role of the media will increase in the 21st century, we must concentrate on creating, through education, discriminating and informed viewers'(Dr Mary Bousted, General Secretary of the ATL).

Teachers and parents

We cannot blame the entire problem of troubled boys on the media. We need to look at our own practices as educators or parents. I am privileged to observe teachers in many classrooms in many schools. There is a huge amount of good practice going on in these classrooms. As teachers we all try to do the best for the children we teach but there are still some practices rife in our schools that cause so many problems to so many boys. The biggest one for me is the issues of criticism. Criticism is a huge issue for boys (Chapter 11), especially for their self-esteem, yet I still come across vulnerable boys being criticized, undermined and humiliated in front of their peers.

Schools that have adopted a policy of 'quiet criticism' are reaping the rewards of this respectful approach. Many schools have implemented Family Links, a wonderful nurturing programme that implements emotional literacy and circle time for all children and *all* staff in schools, supported by a parenting programme and Parenting Puzzle Book (Hunt) with dramatic effects to the well-being of boys, their teachers and their families.

Stressed and tired teachers making flippant comments in front of the class only perpetuate bullying.

Stressed and tired teachers making flippant comments in front of the class only perpetuate bullying, giving other children the licence to treat that child in the same way. Is that boy likely to respect his teacher, let alone go to them for help! One four-year-old boy with ADHD came home from school after his first week and told his mummy, 'I think the teacher only knows my name.' How often was that boy reprimanded? How did that start him off on his journey through school . . .?

As parents many of us are no better. I do believe that each of us tries to do our very best for our children but how does it help if we dress them in T-shirts that give them labels to live up to. The pink T-shirts are likely to have 'Little Angel' or 'Little Princess'. The blue ones 'Little Prince' . . .? More likely I believe to say 'Little Monster' or 'Little Monkey'. Why would Little Prince be unlikely? Is it not acceptable to expect positive behaviours from boys? Would it be likely to see a little girl in a T-shirt with 'Little Cat' with the illustration showing sharp claws? If we say anything against girls it is seen as sexist, it is condemned and is completely unacceptable. I hope that before long it will be as unacceptable to impose negative labels on boys as it is now to tell 'Mother-in law' jokes or to pass racist comments.

It is not just young boys who are labelled. Teenaged boys are labelled as louts, thugs, hooligans, vandals and hoodies in the media and on the streets. Some behaviour may be unacceptable but these generalizations lead to the expectation that all boys behave in this way, it is pre-destined, and boys wearing hoods are to be feared.

The problem with stereotypes is that they are frequently used in a negative way. We are in danger of allowing these to become a self-fulfilling prophecy. Stereotypes, by their sheer nature, are such broad generalizations they do not allow for the fact that each child is an individual. We know, as people who care about the future of boys, that every boy is different, that every boy has his own strengths; we must rise above the media and stereotypes to change the lives of boys for the better.

'Boys will be Boys!' – making it better

Do we believe the stereotypical images as portrayed by the media? I asked parents, teachers and early years professionals, the people who influence boys' lives on a daily basis, to consider 'typical girl behaviour' and 'typical boy behaviour' to see if they hold their own shared perception of how boys behave? This is a useful exercise for assessing the perception of the people close to your boys. It is irreverent and fun but should be taken in the right context. It gives out some stark and powerful messages from which, I believe, we must learn and move forward. As you read on, consider how the shared perceptions of these adults who work and care for children reflect on our boys and the effect their shared perceptions has on their lives.

Little Red Riding Hood

I would like you to imagine a fairy tale. Little Red Riding Hood is going to visit her Grandma who lives the other side of the woods. Little Red Riding Hood has to prepare a basket to take to her Grandma, then journey through the woods to her Grandma's home. In the traditional story, when Little Red Riding Hood arrives at the cottage, her Grandma has either been hidden in the cupboard or been eaten by the wolf (depending on how politically correct your rendition is).

In this version I have taken the liberty of a little artistic licence.

Little Red Riding Hood is a modern-day typical girl; she is allowed to travel to Grandma's cottage, alone (even though social services and the protective parent culture would be unlikely to approve). Her journey does not have to be via the woods, it might be via the high street or the shopping mall and finally, in this version, the wolf has not made it to Grandma's cottage, he is still stuck on the motorway!

What I would like you to consider is what Little Red Riding Hood would do:

- before she left home
- on her journey and
- as she arrived at the cottage

The other twist in the tale is that Little Red Riding Hood had a twin brother: so alongside considering what the typical girl would do in this scenario I would also like you to consider what the typical 'Little Boy Riding Hood' would do:

- before he left home
- on the journey and
- as he arrived at Grandma's cottage

These are just some of the research findings of how Little Red Riding Hood would behave during her visit to Grandma.

Before the Journey
- Change clothes several times making sure they match
- Brush/ straighten/plait and arrange her hair until it is just right
- Look in the mirror

- Think of nice things to go in the basket, possibly Grandma's favourites
- Prepare food for the basket with attention to detail
- Check the list
- Pack a bag for herself with a book, toys, tissues and chocolate
- Listen carefully to mum's instructions
- Check her mobile phone is switched on, charged and has credit, then ring ahead to tell Grandma when to expect her

On the Journey
- Wear flowery wellies carrying her shoes in the basket if it is muddy
- Stay focused on where she is going and plan what to tell Grandma
- Skip, sing and keep clean
- Look at animals and coo
- Pick flowers – pink ones
- Break her nail and make a big drama
- Eat a snack – chocolate
- Run from spiders
- Receive and reply to texts, then gossip on the phone

At the Cottage
- Arrive on time
- Call at the door to let Grandma know it is her
- Tell Grandma how nice she looks and show Grandma her new dress
- Ask how Grandma is, then talk about the journey and herself
- Arrange flowers
- Show Grandma her dance routine
- Show Grandma the contents of her basket, then arrange a tray for Grandma and eat lunch
- Help, fuss and organize Grandma
- Learn crochet

Let us now consider the findings of how Little Red Riding Hood's twin brother would behave during his visit to Grandma.

Before the Journey
- Get up late, ten minutes before he is to leave, then moan and complain
- Wear the clothes he slept in – possibly latest football kit or wear clothes from the floor
- Not wash or clean his teeth
- Play computer game or watch TV until the last minute

(Continued)

Before the Journey — Cont'd
- Prepare nothing for Grandma, his mum or sister will do it
- Be unable to find his belongings, his mum finds his football
- Be asked to leave three times
- Forget his mobile phone – be reminded to take the bag
- Grab his scooter or skateboard and football

On the Journey
- Climb a tree
- Pee on a tree
- Look down – pick up sticks, worms, bugs or stones and get grass stains on his clothes
- Go via sweet shop
- Ride his bike on ramps and hills
- Throw stones in the river and make a dam
- Get hungry and eat a cake from the bag
- Play football with his friend using the bag and his jumper as goal posts and leave his jumper behind

At the Cottage
- Open the door and walk straight in
- Does not wipe muddy feet and leaves footprints on the carpet
- 'Hi' and go to the kitchen . . . 'Can't stop long'
- Ask if there's anything to eat
- Dump his coat and bag on the floor (sandwich is eaten and cake is crushed; present is forgotten)
- Spill coke – not wipe it up
- Quick kiss (if unavoidable) for Grandma, then wipe it off
- Little or no conversation unless about previous day's football
- 'Butter up' Grandma to get money or a treat before he leaves

Stereotypical behaviours

Now consider the following questions for both the boy and the girl.

- Do you recognize some of the behaviours from boys or girls you care about?
- Are the statements mostly positive or negative?
- Which section shows the boy or girl in the best light?
- What are the main characteristics he/she demonstrates here?
- What skills does he/she use?
- From the findings, what adjectives could be applied to boys or to girls?
- Are the behaviours listed seen mostly as positive or negative in the eyes of men?

- Are the behaviours listed seen mostly as positive or negative in the eyes of women?
- Are most of the behaviours seen as:
  o socially acceptable
  o socially desirable
  o socially undesirable
- To what extent do the behaviours include:
  o language
  o physical activity
  o gross motor skills
  o fine motor skills
  o risk taking
  o responsibility
  o planning ahead
  o attention to detail
  o food
  o outdoor activities
  o indoor activities
  o social etiquette
  o technology
- What does this tell us about the common perception of boys/girls?
- If you were male how would you feel about this shared perception of 'the way boys are'?
- If you were female how would you feel about this shared perception of 'the way girls are'?

Whether or not you believe that, as a generalization, boys and girls do behave differently; the Little Red Riding Hood exercise raises some pertinent questions for all of us who care about boys and their future.

In education and in our broader lives the 1975 Sex Discrimination Act resulted in teachers being expected to treat boys and girls in exactly the same way. Differences were no longer allowed. Everyone was worried about saying the wrong thing or being politically incorrect. It was no longer acceptable to line up boys and girls separately, to recruit 'a teacher for boys' games' or to ask for 'some strong boys to help move tables'.

The pendulum swung from some questionable practices, many to the detriment of girls and women, to the extreme where equality was seen as the needs of girls coming first.

Society condemns boys

I believe that Western society condemns boys at every turn. In test results that are seen as so important boys perform badly compared with girls.

'In GCSE in 2006, 54.6% of all boys achieved five or more A*-C grade passes with 64% of girls reaching the same level' (*Times Educational Supplement*, Kirkland Rowell, 4 May 2007).

Boys' behaviour is seen as less than desirable and if, through lack of stimulus and role models they gather in gangs wearing hooded tops they are instantly condemned as 'thugs', 'louts' or 'yobs'. ADHD and Autistic Spectrum Disorders are predominantly found in the male population yet many still dismiss the symptoms of these disorders as deliberately silly behaviour.

The outcome of these shared perceptions, negative images and many social factors has been that, until recently, the needs of boys have been sadly overlooked. Now the Gender Agenda takes over from the Sex Discrimination Act and raises hope that this will begin to address the imbalance for boys.

I have real hope that the Gender Equality Index will not only look out for the needs of women and girls but also help us to begin to look at how little we understand and cater to the needs of boys and men in families, in education, in life. It is down to us to make the difference. To reflect on our current practice and see how we can move forward.

We know, as people who care about the future of boys, that each one has his own strengths, quirks, needs and challenges. We also know that there are some characteristics that are more common to boys than to girls. However, in order to be able to help each boy grow and thrive we need to look past the shared perceptions, the stereotype, past the damning media and generalizations to enjoy the strengths of each child.

We need to get to know each child and his many strands and strengths. Rather than our first response being ABC (Chapter 3).

Anger	The behaviours more likely to be demonstrated by boys are overt, obvious and often less socially acceptable than those of girls. Parents are often worried what others will think; teachers are stretched too thin with large numbers in classes and anger is often our first response.
Blame	There is a feeling in Western society that boys do things to be deliberately disobedient. There is a distinct lack of understanding of the reasons behind why boys may behave in the way they do. Blame is a response that comes very easily, especially when dealing with boys we do not know well.
Condemnation	Following close on the heels of blame comes punishment. 'That'll teach him a lesson.' There are many better ways of helping boys to 'learn lessons' rather than imposing time on a 'naughty step', labelling youngsters or imposing criminal records on boys who would still be seen as children in more open-minded countries.

We need to move further through the alphabet to STUV:

Stop and Smile	We need to *stop* in our busy lives in order to notice this boy when he is being good; we need to catch him before he moves into challenging behaviour; we also need to let him know that we have noticed him and he has our approval. Consider how often we greet troubled boys with a warm smile. It is really worth a try, the difference is vastly disproportionate to the effort. If an incident has occurred, then before we launch in to respond to a boys' behaviour we would benefit from pausing briefly and taking a deep breath. Frequently teachers and parents intervene before it is necessary, especially females. If we stop to take a breath then frequently the issue has resolved of its own accord benefiting both the boy and the adult.
Talk and Think	We need to make time to talk to this boy, to find out what makes him tick as a human being (Daly), not to talk to him as in 'I need to have a word with you' but to chat in the playground, or share a lunch table together, human talking (Chapter 12). This will help us to think before we get angry and condemn; we will be able to match our response to what is going on for that young lad and the results and respect from this approach will be dramatic.
Understand	The body of people who work with boys needs to better understand where boys are coming from. There are many underlying reasons behind why boys behave the way they do . . . testosterone, needs at certain stages in their lives and a legacy from hundreds of thousands of years as a hunter can all impact on the way a boy learns and behaves. Boys themselves will benefit from knowing more about these underlying influences.
Value	We need to value the contributions boys make, focus and develop their strengths and skills. We need to allow boys to do the things they need to but to learn to do them in an appropriate way. We need to Allow, Adapt and Add (Hanen). We then need them to take achievable steps with respectful support towards the areas they are finding difficult (Hemery).

'We need to act rather than react' (Daly).

We need to change our response to boys' behaviours to understand, to be proactive and build in success.

Part 2
Understanding Boys

Testosterone triggers 6

What is it that makes boys different from girls?

This may seem like an obvious question and I'm sure my sons would laugh at me for asking it. Apart from the overt physical differences between the sexes there is something very potent, found in both males and females yet with a much greater influence on boys and men than on their female counterparts ... testosterone.

What does the word testosterone mean to you? What images, feelings or emotions spring to mind? How does it affect our growing men?

What is testosterone?

Testosterone is a steroid hormone from the androgen group. Testosterone is primarily secreted in the testes of males and the ovaries of females although small amounts are secreted by the adrenal glands. It is the principal male sex hormone and an anabolic steroid. In both males and females, it plays key roles in health and well-being. Examples include enhanced libido, energy, immune function and protection against osteoporosis. On an average, the human adult male body produces about eight to ten times the amount of testosterone that an adult female's body does (McBride Dabbs).

'Testosterone is secreted in response to experiences such as stress, fear, aggressive behaviour and sexual encounters' (Siegel et al.).

'Testosterone makes you twitchy and disorganises you' (Biddulph).

These facts are clear and informative but appear to apply mainly to adolescent and adult males.

Testosterone is widely seen to have its greatest effects on boys in the teenage years but it does some of its most powerful work much, much earlier.

Antenatal testosterone surge

Even before a woman may know she is pregnant, a surge of testosterone at around seven weeks of gestation begins moulding the potential boy in her uterus.

One person questioned in my research considered the effects of testosterone to be 'all the growing of all the bits'. She may well have been thinking of those bits we are most familiar with, however, one of the most important bits that testosterone is involved in growing is the brain, in particular, to grow that brain to be able to function specifically as a man. Progesterone and other hormones are involved in this process (Sunderland) but to keep it simple we will focus simply on the testosterone.

The surge of testosterone programmes the brain to invest its growth initially in those areas that will be of most use to a man carrying out the functions that all successful hunting men have been carrying out since man walked the earth. 'Between seven and sixteen weeks is a critical period during which any alterations to the correct amount of testosterone can permanently affect the development of both a boy's sexual organs and his brain' (Macmillan).

Birth

There is a surge of testosterone in boys just after birth. Apart from frequently being born with swollen testicles, this surge seems to have little effect on the external body. The increase in testosterone is seventeen times greater than that in girls, reaching a peak at two months then decreasing to about the same level as in baby girls from about six months.

Could this be to give boy babies the strength to survive in those early weeks or perhaps it is investing even more in the right hemisphere of the brain, enhancing the skills that are more typically male in preparation for the future?

Adolescence

This is probably the age at which we are most aware of the surge of testosterone. Its effects on our teenage boys are very apparent as the physical changes happen almost from one day to the next. The increase in testosterone begins between the ages of eleven and thirteen. (Check out any boys' changing room for this age group and the odours will bear this out!) The physical changes alone are enough to cause insecurity, anxiety and confusing emotions; however this surge of testosterone has an equally strong impact on the teenager's brain, setting it up with a new set of wiring. The increase in testosterone at this age can be as much as 800 per cent (Biddulph). Is it any wonder our growing men turn into the 'Kevin and Perry' characters made popular by the comedian Harry Enfield.

As a woman I find it hard to imagine what an 800 per cent increase in testosterone feels like. One male delegate on my workshops was kind enough to share that at around the age of this testosterone surge, around fourteen, he remembers feeling like he needed to burst. Another male delegate shared with the group that, to him, a testosterone surge feels like 'an icy fury'. If you are an adult male, I hope you feel you can refer to your own first-hand experience, to empathize with our adolescents. If you feel you have little experience of how testosterone makes you feel just imagine having an 800 per cent increase in powerful substance – caffeine. I know that I bounce off the walls if I have had just one cup let alone increasing levels by 800 per cent.

I would suggest that women may have some idea how it feels to have an increase in testosterone levels. Many women do. Apart from the raised testosterone levels triggered by drinking alcohol, I experience the effects of testosterone about once a month. I find myself standing in my kitchen making soup. I have been scratchy with my children, vile to my husband and very short-tempered with the cat. The carrots are being chopped with a vigour (carrot soup is always a favourite at this time) and I feel that I want to throw something. It is only when I get out there on my boys' trampoline and have bounced so high I can see all the neighbours' washing that I begin to feel a little more balanced, less tense, a little calmer.

Most of the time women have levels of oestrogen and testosterone balanced in their bodies. Once a month, in order to trigger menstruation, the oestrogen levels drop making the effects of testosterone feel much more acute. At least Pre Menstrual Tension happens just once a month. I cannot imagine how our teenage boys cope with these feelings and emotions every single day.

Schools and families

What relevance does this have to schools and families? First we need to understand what they may be experiencing. We need to be patient and understanding when our young men are behaving in ways we would rather deny. Biddulph suggests we should, respectfully, support our teenagers as if they were toddlers again, helping them to steer their new bodies and minds in positive directions, helping them to become better organized.

We need to pause before we get angry (ABC Chapter 5) and judge our boys when they lose their homework yet again. This is particularly important in families where their teenage sisters may be equally as stroppy but the contrast in organizational skills is very sharply focused.

Girls are also a big issue at school. Of course we know that but boys cannot help but be attracted and distracted by girls at this age. We need to have systems in secondary schools where girls and boys learn how to respect each other and to co-operate, but also other systems where sometimes boys can learn without the distraction of girls.

> Boys need opportunities to learn without worrying that their every question will end in humiliation in front of the opposite sex.

In education as a whole we have many challenges in the way we schedule the timings of some key events. In secondary school, consider when boys have to make choices about which subjects to study up to sixteen, this decision making happens at a time when he is so confused he cannot decide whether to look for clean socks or just to wear the ones he was sleeping in. Year ten in schools is a big issue for boys. At the age of fourteen boys are stuck in a largely female-oriented education system. Is it any wonder so many of them are excluded?

The contentious subject of testing also causes challenges for boys. SATS at fourteen are likely to show poorer results than we hope for as boys' concentration span is exceedingly short at this age. The tests themselves make things worse as they set up boys for potential failure, especially with tests that match typical girls' learning styles much better than those of boys. Is it surprising

that at the end of the school day many boys can only manage one-word conversations?

There is something to be said for single-sex schooling where the staff is very familiar with the needs of boys, however much more is learned in school than academic subjects making the debate about single-sex schools or single-sex grouping a contentious issue demanding further study and debate.

In research from many workshops the key words that delegates liked with testosterone were: aggression, sex, muscles, anger, strong and macho.

It is strikingly clear how these words link in with behaviours demonstrated by adolescent boys, but do these issues show themselves strongly at any other time in a boy's development?

Four-year-olds

I would like you to reflect on the behaviour typical of boys and girls at around four years old. Since beginning to research this subject several colleagues and I have been observing four-year-old children in many settings with interest.

- Do they play aggressive games?
- Do they act out with aggressive behaviour if frustrated, confused or stressed?
- Are they interested more strongly in 'boy-type' activities . . . fighting, guns, cars, construction?
- Do they have an increased interest in their genitalia?
- Do they show anger in their play?
- Do they get angry with their parents, siblings and peers?
- Do they get angry if things don't go their way?
- Do they use loud voices to show anger, aggression, dominance?
- Do they 'need to move'?
- Do they run around and take up more space than younger children?
- Do they need to move their large muscles?
- Do they find it difficult to use small muscles for fine movement?
- Do they find it difficult to sit still?
- Do they seem to need to kick or punch?
- Do they find it difficult to carry out calm activities for a length of time?
- Do they want to compete to test out their strength/ speed/ skill?
- Do they climb and take risks to test out their developing physical abilities?
- Do they want to be seen as 'manly' or 'macho'?
- Do ANCs encourage them to be big and grown-up, to be tough, not to cry?
- Do they choose to watch fighting programmes on TV?
- Do they choose toys that encourage challenge or fighting?
- Do they wear clothes that make them feel or appear tough?
- Do they demonstrate links to the testosterone-triggered words (Aggression, Sex, Anger, Muscles, Strong, Macho)?

There is disagreement in the research (Biddulph and Macmillan) as to whether there is a surge in testosterone at the age of four. You need to make your own decision and will probably have a fair idea if you have considered the above questions.

I challenged my belief but following much observation and feedback from trusted parents and professionals I do believe there is a surge in testosterone at around the age of four. Whether this is triggered internally from the body's natural programming or triggered by external factors, and the way boys of that age are treated, is a matter for debate. It is most likely to be a combination of the two with one stimulus perpetuating the other. However, if we believe that boys who are four years old demonstrate the testosterone-triggered traits as listed above, this causes us to reflect very carefully on the effects of society's expectations and how we, who nurture, care and educate, treat the four-year-old boys in our care.

Although many things may be going on in the life of a four-year-old boy, I suggest that the biggest impact in his little life so far is the fact that in England (unlike in the majority of European countries) four years old is the age that most boys begin school. How important is it that when a child begins school, in whatever country at whatever age, this experience is a positive one?

What do parents want from school?

- Reading and writing
- Sitting still and listening
- 'Proper' learning rather than 'learning through play'
- Competition – if their child is doing well
- Results in tests and exams
- Academic achievement
- Safe environment
- Sports days and school plays
- Their child to be the best
- Spelling tests and homework
- Schools to do all the work
- Recognizable pictures to bring home each day

This 'wish list' causes a real dichotomy for teachers, particularly for those of four-year-old boys and those in fee-paying settings. Many parents, concerned for their children's futures, mistakenly believe that learning the formalized subjects as soon and as often as possible is the best way forward. It makes parents feel better if they come home with something recognizable on a piece of paper almost as a 'receipt for learning' (Anne Poole, Art and Creativity Consultant).

The very best early years professionals know the huge value of learning through play, creativity and the big outdoors, yet many struggle as the parents who exercise their 'parental preference' have the power to take their children elsewhere or in private education simply to stop paying their salaries.

What are teachers of young children supposed to do? The boys are 'bursting with testosterone' and find it difficult to sit down or even stay in one place for more than a few minutes. This behaviour annoys the girls who label boys as silly or stupid. The parents listen to the messages in the media about low standards for boys and expect their children to learn to read and write at the earliest opportunity but the teacher knows that the boys need to move, run and have freedom to explore.

At the beginning of their school career boys are likely to be approximately a year behind girls of the same age, particularly in literacy and social skills. In Britain it is now suggested that children be kept back if they have not achieved the required levels in year 6. Would it not be better to be proactive – offering parents a choice when a child starts formal schooling, depending on when that particular child is ready for the things school has to offer. This option, if chosen for the right reasons, gives boys a much better start.

> At the beginning of their school career boys are likely to be approximately a year behind girls of the same age.

It avoids boys having to sit next to the little girl who is likely to find fine motor and language skills come easily to her (Chapter 7). When a little boy attempts the same tasks as her he is likely to feel like a failure. (Especially if his birthday is in the summer and hers is in the autumn.) His confidence, self-belief and love of school are destroyed and from the outset he has a negative experience of education. He feels, and in the worst cases is told, that he is no good at school. Not surprisingly he hates it. He is reluctant to go. When he is there he is told off for being noisy, not paying attention and moving around too much. To add insult to injury, the little girl he is sitting next to is not averse to using her superior language skills to tell him how useless he is at every opportunity.

Boys need to be able to exercise their growing, large muscles that may even hurt them if they are forced to sit still. They need to get outside, channel the anger, disperse the aggression, practise their skills and demonstrate their macho tendencies in appropriate physical ways.

> Boys' large muscles may hurt them if they are forced to sit still.

Testing and results cause pressure to teach the 'Three Rs' but if we stick to what boys need most (Chapter 8) in the order they need it for the way their developing male brain is being wired then things will not only be better for boys but for girls, for teachers . . . for everyone.

Testosterone cycles

As I write this it is the school summer holidays. Very soon children will be returning to their classrooms to recommence literacy, numeracy, ICT and whatever foundation and pastoral subjects can be fitted in. They will be expected to sit still, focus, concentrate, listen for prolonged stretches and behave in a socially acceptable manner.

Very soon teachers will be returning to their classrooms to wonder and despair, as I did every autumn for years, at what these terrible parents must have done or not have done with their children during the holidays. (It is amazing how easy it is to blame parents for so much until you actually experience parenthood full on. I'm sure I owe more than a few apologies along the way.) There is bound to be a little mileage in the fact that the children have had freedom and fresh air and then find it difficult to settle to a stuffy classroom. However the fact that boys find it particularly difficult to settle and conform could have some connection with the fact that, in temperate climates, testosterone levels rise in the autumn.

Before you dismiss this fact out of hand, consider humans as mammals. If mammals are living in the wild, when is the best time for their young to be born? In the winter with no food and freezing temperatures or in the spring and summer with better weather and natural food sources readily available. If babies need to be born in the warmer months then simple mathematics based on a nine-month gestation determines that some serious testosterone-driven action needs to take place in the autumn. Hunters would also have needed raised testosterone levels to gather food before the long winter months. Although we hope that our boys in school are not yet off to procreate their gene pool, the length of day and responses to light do have an effect on their testosterone levels.

In temperate climates testosterone levels rise in the autumn.

'Studies have shown conclusively that levels of testosterone, the male sex hormone, are higher in late summer and early autumn than spring, so that's when men have the greatest sex drive and when conception rates are high' (Professor Michael Smolensky, chronobiologist, University of Texas, reported in *The Times Body and Soul Magazine*, 1 April 2006).

Whether or not you take this autumnal pattern of testosterone seriously, its coincidental match with the start of school is not such a happy coincidence.

I doubt that we are likely to change the entire system of school terms based on testosterone levels; however we may be a little more flexible in our understanding of how boys behave.

Before we leave this subject of testosterone I would like to add in one more cyclical fact. This affects boys and men on a daily basis, not just in the autumn. A male's testosterone level rises and falls in a two-hour cycle (Cresswell).

Have you ever experienced asking a boy to do something and felt that the response is less enthusiastic than you had hoped? It may be that his testosterone levels are low or conversely they may be at a peak and he is too 'wired' to be able to focus. Women tend to notice this more than men, perhaps because men know at first hand how the cycles of testosterone affect them and avoid asking at challenging times.

I am not suggesting that we spend our lives tiptoeing around boys waiting until the time is right before we ask anything of them. However if both sexes are aware of this cycle, then a little more flexibility and understanding from both parties can only help.

The power of testosterone

Testosterone has such an impact on the minds, bodies, emotions and well-being of men and boys it is crucial that both men and women gain a better understanding of it. In our mission to make things better for boys we need to be particularly mindful of those boys at the extremes of testosterone continuum.

A boy may have raised levels of testosterone because of things going on around him. Groups of boys together raise the level of testosterone leading to group bravado that would be unlikely in each boy as an individual. It is as if they are swept along in a relentless current.

Aggressive behaviour in itself raises testosterone – consider the Hakka, the dance the New Zealand rugby team perform before their game. This not only raises their testosterone levels but scares the living daylights out of their opponents.

Worry can raise testosterone level focusing the boy into the one thing that is his current priority and an important one for any of us who get angry with our boys . . . anger directed at a boy certainly raises his testosterone level triggering his fight or flight response.

Boys together

Testosterone levels rise when boys get together and the overt emotions such as anger, and aggression transfer quickly from one to another. Dads, especially need to be aware of the contagious effect of testosterone-fuelled emotions, especially if they are prone to get angry with their boys. This can escalate so very quickly until the only outcome of the interchange is two very angry people. Whereas dads still want to be seen as the dominant male they often discipline with the 'tough' approach.

Emotional literacy and strategies to resolve problems are crucial here, both with males and females. There are now so many great workshops for parents (see websites references) where any adult who is prone to demonstrating anger or blame with children can find help and support.

Parents with more than one boy are certainly familiar with this concept ('My house shakes', Louise, mother of six boys). In school teachers need to be aware of this emotion when we group boys in class.

'Boys all working together can be too competitive and not get the job done. It is therefore important to balance out characters, abilities and sexes as appropriate to the task' (Helen, Infant teacher, Ripley Infant School).

Clive, my wonderful family butcher, has years of experience of working with teenage boys in his shop. He will only ever have one boy working with him at once. He tells me this is because they will compete to see who can do the least work.

He quotes, 'If you have one boy you have a good boy, if you have two boys you have no boy at all!'

If this holds true it certainly raises some challenges for all boys and for those of us who teach and care about boys on a daily basis!

High testosterone levels

There are links between high levels of testosterone, aspergers and related autistic spectrum disorders (Baron-Cohen).

Those boys with consistently high levels of testosterone are already going to be apparent to us. They will be demanding our attention through their behaviour and may well be in danger from the drive they have to test things out through challenge and risk taking.

Low testosterone levels

The boys with lower levels of testosterone either temporarily or generally are at risk in our schools and society. Low levels of testosterone can be an indicator of illness, stress, difficulties in their home life. If a boy's behaviour changes then we most definitely need to pay attention and support in whatever challenges he is facing. Boys with generally lower levels of testosterone are often bullied as they are seen not to fit in. They are seen to be weak and challenged by those who feel they are stronger. If they are not in 'the football crowd' or they prefer gentler activities, these boys are often excluded or sidelined.

We need to help these boys discover what they are good at and help them build self-esteem and confidence through praise and positive attention. We need to be sure that all boys are accepted and their skills celebrated wherever they lie on the testosterone continuum. Whether it is because of their age, the season, stresses in their life or influences from others, better results in schools and less stressful relationships in schools and families can be achieved if we all learn to read how testosterone is affecting the boys we care about.

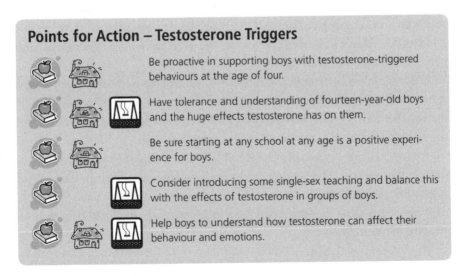

Points for Action – Testosterone Triggers

Be proactive in supporting boys with testosterone-triggered behaviours at the age of four.

Have tolerance and understanding of fourteen-year-old boys and the huge effects testosterone has on them.

Be sure starting at any school at any age is a positive experience for boys.

Consider introducing some single-sex teaching and balance this with the effects of testosterone in groups of boys.

Help boys to understand how testosterone can affect their behaviour and emotions.

7 Brain wiring

The effects of testosterone on the brain

The effects of testosterone are extremely powerful in a growing boy, especially when it comes to the brain. As early as seven weeks of gestation the surge of testosterone begins to prepare the foetus to become a man and in order to do that it invests its energy on the aspects of the brain most suited to helping this child grow into a well-equipped man.

'The human brain is organized essentially like that of our ancestors of fifty thousand and more years ago' (Kimura).

'. . . testosterone initiates a different sequence of brain development than that which occurs in girls' brains (speeding the development of some motor and spatial abilities while slightly slowing the development of other verbal and perceptual abilities)' (Macmillan).

It is certainly not true that every boy is dominant with one brain hemisphere and every girl with the other but there is increasing evidence to support the fact that testosterone does promote the development of the connections in the right hemisphere of the brain from a very early age.

'It (testosterone) gradually changes his brain, shrinking the communication centre, reducing the hearing cortex and growing more cells in the sex and aggression centres' (Brizendine).

Why is this such an important fact in helping us understand how boys develop, learn and behave?

The left side of the brain works with details; it orders things sequentially moving systematically from one step to another. It can follow series of instructions whether in written lists or given verbally. It tends to analyse.

The right side of the brain works with things as large chunks. It is drawn to visual images and the details within those images. (This could account for the fact that boys are usually much happier with non-fiction books or comics where they are drawn to the illustrations and do not have to follow the order of the chapters sequentially.) The right side of the brain functions spatially being able to rotate things to work with three-dimensional shapes. It tends to go with 'gut reactions'.

We already know from studying stereotypes that no two people are the same, whether male or female, so it follows that no two people's brains are exactly

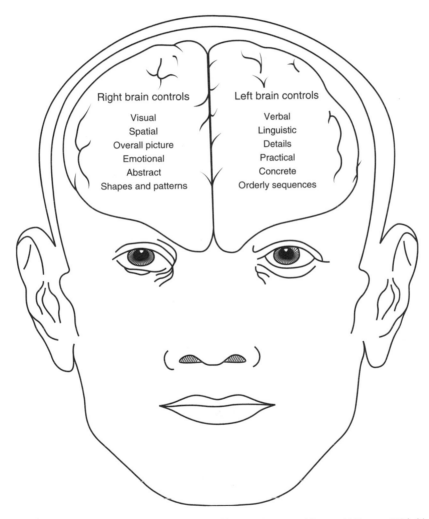

Right brain controls

Visual
Spatial
Overall picture
Emotional
Abstract
Shapes and patterns

Left brain controls

Verbal
Linguistic
Details
Practical
Concrete
Orderly sequences

Moir and Jessel, (1991) *Brain Sex: The Real Difference Between Men and Women*. With kind permission.

the same. Many have tendencies towards the left hemisphere being dominant, others the right hemisphere; some people are fairly equally balanced, however, consider the following:

Does either of the descriptions above better match the way boys you know function?

Does either of the descriptions better match the way teachers you know function?

All human beings, children and adults alike, will have their brains wired in slightly different ways. This will have several contributory factors. Part of it will be down to their gender and whether their brain was developed with the default female blueprint or whether a surge of testosterone changed this development to steer the brain to become that of a man. The strength of this surge and of later surges throughout life will also affect the way the brain's connections are made.

The physical and emotional health of the family that the child is born into and also the environment in which it is raised and nurtured will have a huge effect as will all the learning and experiences through life.

Learning styles

It is important that as educators we research and learn more about how the brain works and how this affects learning styles but it is vitally important that we do not become fixated and narrow our vision to match one specific learning style. We need to use a range of strategies, being open minded to different approaches but particularly questioning the dominance of strategies favouring left-brained learners to the detriment of those with a more right-brained tendency.

Whatever the preferred learning style of each pupil we need to avoid fixing them with labels. It is one thing knowing that you have a tendency towards a certain style of learning but quite another to dismiss all other styles of learning out of hand. As we discovered earlier, labels can be extremely hazardous (Chapter 4).

Whatever the preferred learning style of each pupil we need to avoid fixing them with labels.

Children with predominantly left-brained learning tend to do well in traditional classroom settings; this could be due to the similarity between the left-brained style of many teachers and that of these students. Many teachers, especially females, will need to move out of their comfort zone in order to match the experiences in the learning environment to those children with a more right-brained learning style.

Windham Nursery School, faced with a larger number of boys to girls, looked carefully at how it catered to different learning styles. It provided greater numbers of hands-on investigative activities, many outdoors and many technical including dismantling an old video recorder. The all-female staff, while open minded, benefited greatly from having a male teaching student and learned from his 'subtly different approach, a different voice for storytelling and adding his own interests to our nursery resources'.

Deputy Head Cherry Baker commented that 'the early years practitioners questioned the assumptions that they had made in the past about boys and girls, and the way they did things as female practitioners'.

Although it is really important that we get more good male role models and educators into the lives of boys we need to acknowledge that there are many female practitioners who have a real understanding of what boys need and put this into practice on a daily basis. I wonder how many of us as adults and educators know what style of learner we are. (There are many simple tests for example in *Right-Brained Children in a Left Brained World* (Freed et al.) or in *Why Men Don't Listen and Women Can't Read Maps* (Pease et al.).)

For many years we have been focusing largely on one style of learning in our classrooms. With what we know about brain wiring and development, this seems as ludicrous as expecting a cat and duck to be able to perform the very same tasks with equal success. Maybe in the years to come teaching all children with the same approach will seems ludicrous too.

Although some teachers, schools and parents are still unaware of this issue, I am heartened by the huge breakthrough I have seen in schools in the introduction of VAK – Visual Auditory and Kinaesthetic learning. The impact that considering all three areas in planning activities has, when it is used well, makes a world of difference to all children. It is, in my experience, however the boys who find so much greater success with the introduction of these styles in their learning.

Passion for learning

The very best teachers, as we all know, have made their lessons dynamic, vibrant and with a real purpose for many years. Sadly some of the teaching recently has been stifled by overwhelming paperwork, the need to reach certain standards for inspections and to achieve academic levels for tests.

Those schools confident enough to pursue their passion for active learning have reaped the benefits. One school that has bravely focused on learning through activities, through play, real-life projects, the outdoor classroom and children having real ownerships and vision for their learning have reaped the benefits of outstanding results without having to glue children to desks and extinguish their natural vibrant love for learning.

Another school, Holy Trinity, encourages their staff to pursue their passions. Their teachers have done activities from climbing Everest to sailing across the Atlantic. These activities take more time than school holidays; however, this school has been open minded enough to support these activities, understanding that teachers with a passion and real experiences pass on their love of life and learning to their pupils, alongside coming back to the classroom refreshed and nourished. It is hardly surprising that there is rarely a vacancy at this school, for staff or pupils. The atmosphere there is electric with staff, pupils and parents feeling welcomed and valued.

Parents need to be able to pass on their passions to their children and actively involve 'people with passions' in their children's lives.

We need children to remember what they are learning. As we have discovered the most powerful memories often involve all our senses and engage our emotions. Alongside VAK learning, Sensory and Emotional learning truly engages children and revitalizes tired teachers. (If an acronym is necessary then KAVES would fit the bill.) Emotions are stirred when a child truly engages with a task and has a driving determination because the task really 'speaks to them'. This is why it is vital that schools get to know their boys and their passions so that they can engage with them, beginning with what makes them tick.

> The most powerful memories often involve all our senses and engage our emotions.

Literacy

One of the biggest skills for children to achieve in their infant education is that of literacy. I don't know of an educator or parent who would deny that the skills of listening, speaking, reading and writing are crucial to accessing the world we live in.

What I would question is the vigour and rigour with which some schools and even nurseries try to force feed reading and writing onto children who are not yet ripe enough to be receptive for it. Steve Biddulph (at Secondary Headteachers' Conference 2000) says we form our attitude to education in the first three to six months of school.

If we introduce boys to literacy tasks when they are not ready for them, this in itself can place them under stress. When a child is under stress they are likely to revert to the more basic brain functions, the fight-flight responses frequently cut in. Under stress there is less cross brain work and more single hemisphere work, the hemisphere used more readily by that child. Therefore if you have got a boy who is particularly right brained, when he is put into a situation where he is expected to try language tasks he is not ready for, his response to this stress will make it more difficult for him to perform that task successfully. This will likely lead to a feeling of failure and feeling 'useless'.

It is so sad that with many boys language and literacy skills are approximately six months behind that of girls at this stage that they are put into situations where they feel failures and this is the pattern that so frequently follows them through their school career.

The way that testosterone impacts on the brain and the differing location of areas for language mean that girls have areas for language in both hemispheres of their brain. Boys have them in just one hemisphere, the left, and as we know this is the hemisphere that is typically less developed in boys.

'Scans also showed . . . a difference by gender that had not been found before . . . in areas of the brain that are responsible for reading, language, emotion and behaviour.

'In males, the temporal lobe and the deep cerebral region of the brain are preferentially affected' (Allan L. Reiss, MD, Department of Psychiatry, Stanford University . . . reported on BBC news, 8 August 2004).

It is not that the two hemispheres are of different sizes; it is simply that one side will have more connections; on MRI scans this will show up as more folds.

MRI scans taken of premature boys show that the left side of the brain frequently has few folds, the right side having many more.

Corpus callosum

Brain research has only really taken off in the last ten years now that MRI scans can show the activity in the brain.

Although a boy's brain is typically bigger than that of a girl, the amount of connections, especially between the two hemispheres is much less. This does not mean that a girl's brain is superior, simply that boys and girls' brains make connections in different ways.

> A girl's brain is not superior, it is simply that boys and girls' brains make connections in different ways.

If you imagine a girl's brain, with two fairly equal hemispheres, just as with people, if two people are equally developed or intelligent, they are likely to communicate forming links. In boys one side of the brain is much more developed than the other offering many fewer opportunities for the two sides to work together, fewer connections as they are not yet equal partners.

These connections, rather like threads, are called the corpus callosum. It is hardly surprising that the corpus callosum is much more developed in girls than in boys as their brain is developing in a balanced way that encourages communication between the two hemispheres. In fact a girl's brain is developing in a way that it encourages communication full stop. Also girls have centres for language and other skills in more than one hemisphere making it easier for them to multi-task. Boys have their language centre only in the left hemisphere – a possible reason why they find it so hard to listen to more than one thing at once.

Typically boys also find it much easier to do one thing at once. This is often joked about but it is a serious consideration if we are teaching or living with boys and frequently ask them to do something when they are focusing on another task. It is also important for boys to know that multi-tasking is an area they find difficult. We are not looking for excuses, after all focusing on one thing has great merit, what we are looking for is ways to help boys to cope when they are in situations where doing more than one thing at once is necessary.

In a boy's brain the spatial, visual physical areas are typically much more developed than communication so the language facility comes considerably later. The links with ADD are strong in this area. Freed et al. state that 'all ADD children are right brained and have a visual learning style'. In typically right-brained learners they see the whole picture, then fill in the detail; those whose left brains dominate work with details and build them up into the whole picture.

Palmer suggests that children who are exposed to too much TV under three years have an increased risk of ADD and ADHD. I would suggest that the visual input of television is so strong that much more focus is given to this area of the brain to the detriment of links with the left side so crucial for language.

It has been said of toddlers that they will 'either talk or walk'. Especially with boys it is rare to find toddlers who take off with their talking and walking at the same time. One does take priority and in boys who are typically right brained the physical activity is much more likely to come first.

Language

'Men are dial up, women are broadband.'

In the classroom, in the home, which sex typically does the most talking? Girls and women solve problems by talking; boys and men solve problems by being quiet. How often do boys get told off in schools for 'not paying attention'? Next time you are tempted to leap in when a boy is being quiet or taking a long time to answer a question, look at the body language, the facial clues. Could it be that this boy is working through the solution in his head and will get there better without interruption from us, the adults?

Boys and men are more likely to talk about one subject and stick with it. If they pause to think they find it most frustrating if someone interrupts, filling the gap. It is difficult for them to regain their train of thought. Girls and women are used to juggling several threads of conversation at once. They happily interrupt each other and are interrupted. Males in this environment find this style of conversation difficult and frequently impossible to understand. A delegate on the 'Making It Better for Boys' workshop described the difference in style as 'men are dial up, women are broadband'.

Males use far fewer words than females; one estimate is that including gestures, adult males speak on average 7,000 words a day while women are closer to 18,000 words. Apart from the difference in phone bills, it is important that we focus on this discrepancy in our day-to-day encounters.

Females also talk around a subject while males are concise and to the point. This can cause misunderstandings between the sexes. If a teacher or parent asks a boy 'Can you do up your laces?' there is a strong chance she is simply expecting him to tie them up. A boy, especially if he is feeling sensitive may interpret this as 'Are you capable of tying up your laces?' which is questioning his ability. Instructions are much more effective put respectfully or using words such as will and would rather than can or could.

David Hemery, ex-Olympic athlete, has studied the use of language in coaching, much of which is with boys. He suggests that rather than giving commands or instructions we should use a questioning approach, 'Is there a better place to put your coat?' This gives responsibility to the boy, trusting him to solve the problem. He then needs to think it through, building good brain connections for himself, before finding the solution.

There are times and places to 'tell' but we must use this device sparingly.

If we simply tell boys what to do we are missing out on opportunities for learning and we need to seize these wherever and whenever possible.

I experience being told what to do when I tap in a postcode to my satellite navigator. It gets me to schools and venues without having to stop in the middle of the one-way system. This really serves my purpose as I want to think about the content of my presentation rather than improving my geographical skills. It gets the results but teaches . . . nothing!

Telling boys what to do can be helpful in times of stress or when they have absolutely no idea of how to solve this particular problem but it always needs to be done respectfully. We need to encourage and support boys in solving problems themselves. I suggest many parents and teachers do *tell* boys what to do, often much more than is necessary, especially when tired, busy or stressed. It makes for an easy life . . . in the short term! Think back to the Red Riding Hood exercise. Many of the challenges the boy faced in getting ready to go to Grandma's are skills he needs to learn for life. So many delegates said that mum or sister did the jobs for him. Do parents and teachers expect less of boys in families, in nurseries, in schools?

People often wonder why boys don't do things first time they are asked. Could it be . . .

- There is too much waffly language?
- The child hasn't heard you? (He is effectively deaf when engrossed in a task. He can only hear one thing at a time.)
- He got distracted by something more interesting?
- Someone else always does it if he leaves it?
- He usually gets asked at least five times so he may as well wait for the time when you REALLY mean it?
- He'd much rather play with the cars (he's good at this) rather than having to do hand-writing practice (which he hates)?
- He has glue ear? Many boys suffer from this especially if they are having a growth spurt.
- He is experiencing stress and this affects the way he thinks and responds?
- His blood sugar is low; all he can think of is food?

On a 'boys' workshop a teacher of a reception class asked for our help. She has a group of four-year-old boys 'who won't sit still and listen in story time'.

The delegates asked some questions . . .

- How long is story time?
- What time of day is it?
- Where do the children sit?

The story time was for twenty minutes directly before lunch. Thirty hungry children sat on the carpet and the female teacher reads fairy tales.

From what we know already of four-year-old boys we know that they need to move around. Sitting still for twenty minutes would be a real challenge. The subject material needs to be well chosen to capture and keep the boys' interest. Listening without actions or movements for this length of time would also be a challenge as their brains are less tuned in to listening than girls let alone that their bodies know they need food, let alone that blood sugar levels would have dropped making concentration even harder. Food is their main focus. If boys are thinking of food and find difficulty multi-tasking then food will win out. The teacher reported that the boys kept looking towards the side door to the classroom rather than towards the front of the group. It emerged that this is the door used by the lady who takes them to dinner each day.

The teacher made plans to go back to school and re-assess her story time.

Liz Lander, a senior lecturer from Roehampton University, encourages her student teachers to think less about behaviour management and more about motivation. 'If we motivate our children to be involved and engaged in the tasks then there will be far fewer behaviour management issues to deal with.'

I suggest with increased knowledge about reasons why boys may behave the way they do; we can begin with understanding, understanding of where the behaviour is coming from then be better placed to motivate with well-matched teaching and activities. We need to be proactive and positive to make things better for everyone.

Special needs

Why is it that boys are more likely to have special needs than girls? Consider the birth process, not a breeze for either party but especially a little boy. He is larger than a little girl and also his head is larger so there is more chance of him having a difficult time making his way into the world. (Perhaps is this why there is a testosterone surge at this time to help him have a fighting chance? (Chapter 6).)

Most babies born suffer some brain damage, perhaps this would be better described as brain distress.

The human body is amazing in its healing powers so most of this 'distress' is easily healed; however, consider if a little boy has damage to the right side of his brain during birth. This side is fairly well developed and the testosterone at birth would help to promote healing in this area. If a little girl suffers damage to her right hemisphere, this is fairly well developed and again would heal relatively easily. Consider the left hemisphere. In a little girl this is also fairly well developed and would therefore repair readily in most cases. What if damage is caused to the left side of a little boy's brain? This side is much less developed than the right. It has comparatively few connections so if there is damage to this side, the side solely responsible for language in most boys, then what might the results be?

Consider a typical special needs group of children aged about six years old. How many of these special needs are for language? How many of the children in these groups are boys? Do you see a possible link emerging?

Not only is boys' language development months behind that of a typical girl but also these boys may well have suffered some damage to the language side of their brain either at birth or at an early age.

Many physical things have to be in place for these boys before their language will ever have a hope of being successful in the way that formal education and testing requires (Chapter 8). Fortunately, the connections necessary for these skills to be developed will come . . . when the brain begins to work consistently across the hemispheres.

Dyslexia and reading

Dyslexia is found more frequently in boys than in girls. Boys who are dominant with their right brain see words as pictures; their strengths are in the visual rather than in small steps, breaking things down, phonics, more typical skills for reading. This visual dominance can help explain why many dyslexics find it difficult to differentiate between the letters b and d. If they were to see a cat walk between two bushes from left to right it would be a cat! If a few minutes later that same cat were to walk between the two bushes from right to left it would still be a cat. The dyslexic sees it as a visual image and has used his spatial skills to rotate that image as the cat walks back. It therefore makes sense in the dyslexic mind that when a group of straight lines and curves is one way it is the letter b and rotated it is also the letter b. This knowledge does not immediately overcome their dyslexia but it does help us to understand some of the stumbling blocks between these children and learning to read. It could explain why the visual and kinaesthetic approach to learning phonics called 'Jolly Phonics' has been so successful.

> If a few minutes later that same cat were to walk between the two bushes from right to left it would still be a cat!

It is of utmost importance that adults read to boys. Technology and time pressures have pushed this activity aside. Reading with your boy will help to give him a love of language, a love of books. If boys see that we give books a priority then they will also see it as 'the thing to do'. It is especially important that boys see their dads or respected men reading. So many more boys are likely to see their role models at a computer or on a console game these days. The other lovely thing about parents reading with their children is it gives an excuse for snuggling up close and having some calm, physical contact. This in itself boosts their self-esteem, well-being and even helps to build positive brain connections.

It is of course important to talk to boys, to help and encourage them to talk to us and to their peers, even though they may well be less inclined than their female counterparts.

> 'Speech difficulties are a growing problem among the "video generation"' (ICAN).

It is important to use specific and descriptive language, especially when it comes to describing emotions and feelings. Emotional literacy is so powerful in the lives of young boys. The Family Links Nurturing Project (Hunt) has made a real difference to the lives of many children, their teachers and families. It is run in classrooms with workshops for parents alongside these. It empowers children to think about their feelings and offers them appropriate language to be able to express them without resorting to fists or aggression.

For boys emotion is based in the right side of the brain, language on the left, so offering them many opportunities to make the links between these two centres is crucial. We know that boys need the skills of a typical man but we are living in a world where really good communication skills are paramount.

Brain gym and behaviour 'disorders'

Brain gym goes a long way in addressing the needs of boys. It is a very powerful tool often reserved for children with special needs but of huge value to all children.

It works on a physical basis with exercises helping the body to make connections that in turn help make connections in the brain. It can help with good brain development, relieving stress, as well as having a huge impact on children with language delay or 'behaviour disorders' such as ADHD, autism and aspergers.

Although there is no definitive method for diagnosing ADHD, Tom Daly in *How to Turn Any Disruptive Child into Your Best Student* suggests nine possible traits of ADHD children.

- Are hard to like
- Need unlimited amounts of attention
- Cannot handle unstructured free time
- Have big gaps in their achievement
- Have no concept of age-appropriate personal space
- Exhibit serious or dangerous behaviours
- Only learn things intermittently
- Need to relearn school procedures over and over
- Seem to have a 'faulty connection'

The Hyperactive Children's Support group also has some really useful material on diagnosing and supporting children with ADHD and autistic spectrum disorders.

These disorders are closely linked to testosterone and how it shapes the brain; in fact Simon Baron-Cohen in 'The essential difference' refers to autism as 'the extreme male brain'. Many of the strategies suggested for supporting children with autistic spectrum disorders also work well for boys who may be right brain dominant. Although there is no blood test or specific criteria against which to measure ADHD it is believed that the following well-known people have it: Jamie Oliver, Sir Winston Churchill, Sir Richard Branson and in the past Sir Isaac Newton and Albert Einstein. If ADHD and its close relatives on the autistic spectrum are *disorders* then how come so many of the men above have received honours?

We need to see the positives in the behaviours of these 'disorders' and help the children with these to have good experiences at home, in society but crucially in schools.

Some other 'snapshot' facts about the brain that contribute to the picture we are building come from Michael Gurian *The Minds of Boys*.

- Male brains tend to produce higher levels of dopamine in the bloodstream than girls. This affects impulse control and makes it harder for boys to learn while sitting still.
- The neural connectors in the sense memory and listening centres of male brains tend to be weaker than those in girls. Boys therefore absorb less information verbally than girls, and are more stimulated by visual and tactile input.
- Male brains get about 15 per cent less blood flow than female brains. To compensate, brain activity is compartmentalized which means boys tend to fare better when able to focus on a single task.
- Male brains like to go into a rest state between tasks, which is characterized by reduced neural activity. A female brain 'at rest' is much more neurally active than a male brain.

If we have questions concerning whether testosterone does affect the way our human brains develop then we should consider the following:

In 1992 a sex change patient was making the transition from being female to being male. After three months of testosterone treatment 'he' began to view the world differently and think differently.

'I have problems expressing myself, I stumble over my words. Your use of language becomes less broad, more direct and concise. Your use of words changes, you become more concrete . . . I think less, I act faster, without thinking.

The visual is so strong . . . when walking in the streets I absorb the things around me. I am an artist, but this is so strong. It gives a euphoric feeling. I do miss, however, the overall picture. Now I have to do things one at a time; I used to be able to do different things simultaneously.

I can't make fine hand movements anymore; I let things fall out of my hands. My fantasy life has diminished strongly . . . unfortunately I would have liked to keep that. I am becoming more clumsy, more blinkered. I didn't ask for this; it just happens' (Van Goozen (1994) in McBride Dabbs).

8 Knowing what boys need – physical development, respect and responsibility

Building your bike . . .

A boy is like a bike. It may look perfectly built, ready to take on the task for which it is designed but with closer inspection we may find that it is not that stable; some of the connections are not yet in place. Some joints need a little more attention before they are ready to take the strain and travel forward in life.

Imagine a bicycle that has been very carefully assembled but is still extremely fragile. Many of the connections are difficult to see but they have not been tightened up and some still need to be put in the right places. If we expect that bike to work fully as a bike we are going to be disappointed. If we are pedalling it forward we may come to a sticky end; we may get hurt and the bike may well get damaged.

This is exactly what can happen to boys if we push them on to the 'next thing' without really knowing and respecting them as individuals and taking the time to understand which piece of their bike is next in line for bolting together . . . which bit needs your attention.

This simple analogy helps us to look at boys more carefully, especially at vital ages and stages in their lives. It is so important that we are not bound by systems and text books that tell us the exact age that boys must do things whether that is starting school, learning to read or becoming a man. We know there are systems in place that rule our lives but we need to know when they are working for us and when to challenge them. When we really know the boys we teach or care about we will know when they are ready for the next step along the journey and when the systems and people around them are able to work together to make each 'next step' a positive and successful one.

> We know there are systems in place that rule our lives but we need to know when they are working for us and when to challenge them.

Building up boys, bit by bit

If I were to pass you my precious new-born son and I knew that you had never held a baby before what would I be most likely to tell you? To support the head. It seems obvious.

When they are first born babies have little or no control of their limbs or muscles. The muscles in the neck are not yet ready to support the head. We need to support it for them. Gradually the boy builds up strength, connections are made in his body and his brain and he can hold up his head unsupported. We know this. Every adult who has ever had a baby or worked with them knows this . . . but do we know which connections are made next? After the head and neck the connections continue to be made through the torso. Cecilia Armour, training coaches at 'Kidsports' described this development as 'Cranial-Caudal Proximal-Distal'.

Cranial-Caudal Proximal-Distal development

In order for these connections to develop well the baby has to have opportunities to develop their strength. They need to spend more time flat to develop their neck and core stability. This core stability enables the brain, communication and co-ordination to work better. Babies need to spend as little time as

possible in constraining 'bucket' seats or buggies that restrict their movement. They need to spend time on their fronts in order to build strength in their shoulders. (This stage has been missed out for many babies due to the advice given to prevent cot death.) There was a whole generation of babies around the mid-nineties who spent most of their little lives in car seats with little time to stretch out and frequently with their car seat parked in front of the Teletubbies. I suggest we may be reaping the rewards from this with the many challenges this generation of children is facing.

When the cranial-caudal links are all in place then the connections begin to be made from where the large limbs meet the body out towards the fingers and toes. This is called proximal-distal. These connections are made slowly and steadily, benefiting from opportunities to use the large muscles as they develop in strength. Children need to be able to move around, especially boys whose connections come later than in most girls.

At the age of four, when many children begin school, boys are still developing connections in their large muscles. They need whole arm movement; they need whole leg movement. They need to move. It can actually be painful for a boy if he is not allowed to move while these large muscles, their nerves and connections are developing. Girls, having more connections between the hemispheres in their brains, typically complete this physical development earlier than boys, and while they still need opportunities for exercise they are already beginning to develop the connections to their fingers and toes. They can carry out fine motor activities and achieve success, threading, cutting, sticking and holding a pencil. Boys will not be ready to develop these fine motor connections until the gross motor connections and core stability are well established.

Sallianne, manager of a day nursery, decided to test out this theory. She set up a range of activities some using fine motor skills and others gross motor skills. She allowed the children aged three to four in her setting to choose their activity with no guidance or direction. Time after time the boys went to the large wall painting and the girls to the threading. One girl joined in with the wall painting for a while and occasionally boys would go to the bead table but only stay there a matter of seconds.

> Time after time the boys went to the large wall painting and the girls to the threading.

Until we have allowed them to run, use big paint walls, throw things and generally take up more space they are lacking the foundations on which to build. This may not happen until a boy reaches seven years of age.

Perhaps when we next look at what we are expecting boys to achieve, especially between the ages of four and seven, when their colouring looks like a hurricane at sea, we will understand that we can make them hold a pencil and write 'C' shapes until the cows come home. Some may be ready but those that aren't will benefit much more from being allowed to make 'C' shapes with large arm movements, on walls, in the air, in sand, on their friend's back, anywhere big but certainly not by sitting at a desk next to Chloe.

Brain gym exercises take the large 'C' shape further and use it to develop strong links across the corpus callosum. This method encourages 'lazy eights' developing a smooth flow in the hand movement and crossing the hemispheres in the brain. Brain gym is fabulous for all children but especially boys and those with autistic spectrum disorders (Hannaford).

In many countries where formal education begins at six or even later the struggles do not arise and amazingly enough when the children are ready for the fine motor work it comes so much more easily leaving the child's self-esteem intact as well as the parents' and teachers' frayed nerves.

Chris, an experienced educator, had done no formal research into how the brain develops and how physical development occurs in boys; however her observations of the boys she cares for were as follows:

'They are out of this planet in maths and science, the technical side and logic. They struggle in reading, writing and spelling. They hit seven and it all just clicks into place.'

If only I could reassure all those parents who are worried that their boy is six and he is still not reading. We now know that the physical has to be in place before the fine motor can begin to be effective, only then can the typically male brain give its energies to the left hemisphere and connections between the two to invest in the skills necessary for reading, writing and spelling.

When my eldest son was struggling with reading around the age of six, Shirley, an experienced, paediatric physiotherapist, shared with me this pearl of wisdom . . .

'When they can skip they are ready to read'.

'When they can skip they are ready to read.'

Check out the theory; see how many of the children you care about begin to take off with reading when they have enough brain connections and co-ordination for the complex task of skipping. If this holds true then it is hardly surprising that girls, who can't stop skipping, take off with reading so much earlier than boys.

Raising the next generation of boys . . . who is responsible?

'There is no greater responsibility than raising the next generation.'

This is the quote from one of the most important documents to be published in recent years, the Respect Action Plan.

One of the problems with raising the next generation is that no one seems to be prepared to take responsibility and everyone, including the youngsters themselves, is quick to place the responsibility onto others.

Teachers

Since the introduction of the National Curriculum in 1988 teachers have been under attack. They have received a barrage of demands, changes and criticism. This was closely followed by The Children Act in 1989, SATS in 1990, Ofsted and its name and shame policy in 1992, then a whole rash of updates revisions, literacy, numeracy. . .. The list goes on. If schools are being charged with raising the next generation, are they being trusted to actually know the children they are working with and have some professional integrity?

I remember at the beginning of testing, I heard many colleagues stating plainly that they would not be teaching to the tests. There are very few schools now that don't. All but the bravest have to teach to the tests to get the results to keep them in a strong place in the league tables.

I believe that many teachers have become impotent. Any passion for teaching struggles to surface beneath the regular tidal waves of tests, inspections and teaching the same lessons in the same way at the same time.

> We have to get the passion back into teaching, back into our schools.

When I observe trainees in school I always try to avoid visits in the morning. The lesson is either literacy or numeracy and with a few exceptions it is taught in the same way to the same formula. This is what is expected of so many teachers today. I feel for them. Formulaic teaching turns me off! The teachers often feel uninspired and strait-jacketed, so is it any wonder the kids get turned off, especially the boys who need dynamic teaching to keep them engaged?

Mothers

Mothers are now expected to work as well as run fabulous households. Mothers are blamed for having their children when they are too young or they are too old. Mothers are blamed for feeding their children fast food, for feeding their babies formula, for mollycoddling their children, for giving them too many toys, for returning to work too soon (even though government encourages it). Being a parent is a day-to-day guilt trip without being worried that whatever you do is wrong.

> Lone mothers need our help and respect, not our criticism.

If mothers in two-parent families feel criticized, consider single mums. If you attend the press it seems that if you are a lone mother bringing up a boy you might as well book his place in Broadmoor now. You have absolutely no hope. You struggle to make ends meet, get blamed if you work and leave your kids, blamed if you don't work, blamed if you over-protect your boy, blamed if you don't know where he is, blamed if you do not have a father figure in your son's life and blamed if you seek male company. One delegate on a recent 'Mothering Sons' programme for lone parents described being the single mother of a son as 'a chaotic jungle'. There is no denying it is extremely hard work for any lone parent to bring up a son but lone mothers need our help and respect, not our criticism.

Fathers

Fathers, as mothers, are now expected to be successful in at least two roles. They are expected to provide financially for the family as well as being hands on, touchy feely, with the children, cook pasta and coach the local football team. They are criticized if they work long hours; they are frowned upon if they don't work. They are expected to provide the latest gadgets for their off-spring and criticized if they can't.

Absent fathers may as well line themselves up in the stocks and let any passing woman throw rocks at them.

It does seem to be that it is acceptable for women to talk publicly about how terrible men are, yet, if a man were to speak about a woman in the same way that women speak about men he would be shouted down for being sexist. Certainly, we would all prefer it if families stayed together and lived happily ever after but life isn't always like that. We need to help and support families in crisis and if it is possible to resolve the differences and help more relationships to survive. We need to make life easier for families so that the stresses do not build up. We also need to make life better for absent fathers and help them in their relationships with their children, their boys, by supporting them and not berating them. There are now many organizations and parenting networks offering support, advice and activities specifically for dads (see website references).

If it isn't the parents who are to blame or the schools, who is responsible for raising the next generation of boys? Is it the boys themselves? We do leave a lot of decision making to the children these days; they have so many choices, but are they ready for this responsibility? Do we actually teach them how to take responsibility? If the media and internet are acting as their parents where do they get a feeling of security and stability? How do they feel safe? If boys do things wrong we punish and condemn them but are they mature enough to take responsibility? Are they being expected to grow up too soon?

Communities

If you are an adult with no children do you have responsibility for the next generation? I suggest you do.

> We all hate crime and poverty.

All of us have to live with the results of children's actions, the majority of anti-social behaviours being carried out by boys, who lose their way in education or in families. We all hate crime and poverty, however we have no right to complain about the state of the local community unless we are actively participating, in however small a way, to make things better. There is an old African saying 'It takes a village to raise a child'. We do not live in Africa, nor necessarily in a village; however, we all have the opportunity to replicate all the best things about villages if each and everyone of us puts in just a bit more effort.

Raising great boys

Bringing up boys should be a positive experience for parents, for teachers, for families, for boys themselves. I am not looking at the world through rose-tinted glasses. It is really important that we all have the opportunity to experience life and learning in a positive way. Recent neuoroscientific research shows us the effects that positive (and negative) experiences have on the brain (Sunderland).

If we regularly receive positive experiences in babyhood it primes our brain to be more receptive to positive experiences in life and to be able to draw on these when the going gets tough. This is due to a cocktail of hormones especially oxytocin.

If a baby boy has few positive experiences then the brain is not primed towards positives in later life, it actually leaves more space for receptors to cortisol, a hormone closely linked to adrenalin and stress (Further reading: *Cortisol in the Early Years*, Balbernie). The stressful times then are seen to be much bigger, more important and take much longer to get over. We all experience disappointment, sadness, anger and stress but the most important thing in life is how we deal with them. We so often see the outcomes of boys' anger, stress and depression, being able to rationalize and control these stresses and emotions is a vital, powerful tool. The more oxytocin receptors boys have in their brains the better they can handle the stresses.

> If we experience positive experiences in babyhood it primes our brain to be more receptive to positive experiences in life.

While it is crucial that babies have positive experiences to set them up for life it is never too late. Workers with looked-after children have seen that with just two weeks of having an adult show they care, with a one-to-one relationship and positive experiences, this is enough to make a difference to how these teenagers move forward in their lives. They will always have the memory of those positive experiences to draw on and more than the memory, those positive experiences have actually changed the way the brain works, how it experiences positives and how it deals with stress. For this child the stresses will now feel just a little smaller.

Points for Action – Knowing What Boys Need

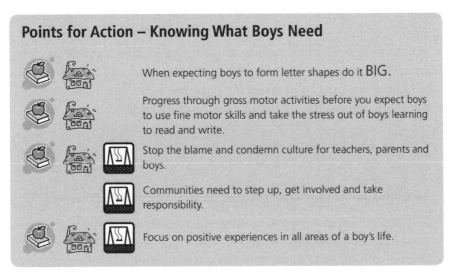

When expecting boys to form letter shapes do it BIG.

Progress through gross motor activities before you expect boys to use fine motor skills and take the stress out of boys learning to read and write.

Stop the blame and condemn culture for teachers, parents and boys.

Communities need to step up, get involved and take responsibility.

Focus on positive experiences in all areas of a boy's life.

9

Who do boys need?

Zero to six – filling the 'Mummy-shaped gap'

From the moment a child is born the power of physical human contact is immense. A child can be cared for in all other meanings of the word but if they do not receive caring human touch there is a large gap.

Rene Spitz, an Austrian-born psychologist in the mid-twentieth century wrote, 'Infants that are not hugged and touched, even if they have food and clothes, suffer from retarded neurological development.'

Appropriate physical touch, especially skin on skin, triggers a feel good sensation. The Family Links Nurturing Programme (Hunt) calls this feeling 'warm and fuzzy'. Apart from being a wonderful feeling, this sensation promotes the development of receptors in the brain, those that receive oxytocin, the positive brain chemical. Put simply, the more receptors a child develops for oxytocin (positive) the less space there is for receptors that receive cortisol (negative).

'Oxytocin is produced by loving touch, being held by a parent or caring person. This is crucial in early life' (Sunderland). Apart from being the healthiest option for a baby, breast feeding offers all of these vital opportunities plus eye contact and good attachment with the mother.

A baby needs 'warm and fuzzy' experiences.

In these early years a baby needs to get as many 'warm and fuzzy' experiences as possible and few 'cold and prickly' negative experiences. They need to be touched, smiled at, cooed at, have eye contact made, be rocked, be sung to, be read to, be mimicked, in fact be a very special person to the person who is giving the care. Margot Sunderland calls this 'delighting'.

Why is this particularly pertinent to boys?

Dr Kraemer of the Tavistock Clinic and Whittington Hospital in London (2000) says 'Parents need to show more affection to baby boys. Lack of affection could result in boys struggling throughout their lives from school to depression to suicide'.

Girl babies automatically engage more with the human face. They give lots of eye contact sustained for longer periods than boys and they are more likely to babble. This all means that there are many more opportunities for this 'delighting' to happen with little girls.

I find it hard to believe that I could have spoken to a baby more than I did to my boys but I understand that, had my beautiful boys been gorgeous girls, I would have used language even more with them. Not only this but with the language centre in only one part of the male brain (Chapter 7) parents need to seize every possible opportunity to immerse boys in language and help them develop a love for words stories, poems and songs.

Delighting is not restricted to sounds. If a child pats a soft toy, we need to pat the soft toy too and then it becomes a game. When someone respectfully copies us or shows an interest it can often give us that tingly feeling, the rush of oxytocin over the brain. They have bothered to take time for us; they are showing us that they care.

> Delighting gave me a licence to play to blow bubbles in the bath, to make train noises at meal times and simply adore my toddler.

Pat-a-cake and train noises were things I had done, as I'm sure all parents have, but I had never known the reasons they were so important. The very best mums, those who don't need to know the reasons, have believed in pat-a-cake and so much more for generations. My own mother would have laughed at me writing this. When I look back she knew all of this and did it without a second thought. Thanks Mum. She never knew about oxytocin and cortisol. She used her gut feelings as millions of mums have done effectively for generations. People with these innate skills are often those who choose to become childminders. They will be able to do what they love most as a job. If only everyone was that lucky.

> Mums have used their gut feelings effectively for generations.

Mothers and the parenting role have been undervalued for decades. How often have you heard a woman say 'I'm just a mother'?

The problem we have today is that many mums are in isolation. It is less likely that grandparents, aunts and uncles will be living close by to offer support.

Even with a father around they can spend days alone with their babies and toddlers. It is boring; all adults need stimulation and support from other adults.

One respected childminder in Croydon reported that 'Parents who have family nearby giving support seem much more relaxed than isolated families with no support but books'.

I suggest that we learn from the good work of groups such as Homestart and National Childbirth Trust both informing, supporting and 'looking out' for parents of young families. I believe every expectant mother should be matched to a caring local volunteer whose role is similar to the one that used to be taken by extended family. This person could be considered a 'Lookout'. She would have backup and training from health visitors and midwives but more importantly she would be a friendly face, a listening ear, a little adult company who can be on hand when times are tough and be there to share smiles and successes.

Working mums

Some mums go back to work at the earliest opportunity, they may need to financially, for their career progression, for their own sanity or simply because they have the choice. Whoever the parents choose to care for their child it is so important that the person caring for that child sees them as very special; they need to know that their care of that child is the foundation for life. It establishes patterns on which the rest of their lives and learning are built.

The care does not have to be given by a woman but as Sue Palmer puts it the carer needs to fill 'a mummy-shaped gap'.

Wherever the child is cared for he needs to know that he is special and that he is loved.

We need to support mums who choose to stay at home just as we need to support mums who choose childminders, nannies and nurseries.

Both Biddulph and Sunderland make strong cases against nurseries for the under threes referring to the stress it can cause young children. I have experienced many different practices in nurseries and would encourage you to be informed and to make your own decisions based on your knowledge and what you see.

'Too much repeated stress and failure to shut down after stress . . . can have an immediate effect on the heart, the brain and immune systems' (Siegel et al.). 'Adrenalin cuts in to cause short term protection but in the long term this can cause damage; over time this can lead to a loss of neurons in the brain.'

I have run countless workshops for nurseries and have been heartened by the commitment so many of them have made to overcoming challenges that can make it so difficult for them to fill that 'Mummy-shaped gap', minimize a young child's cortisol (stress) levels and have the understanding to welcome boys and their behaviour positively.

I have great respect for Susan Green, a nursery owner as, following the 'Boys' workshop she completely reviewed the practice in her chain of nurseries. They now have a policy to reflect 'The Home Environment' and her staff speak of the huge difference it has made to them, the boys and girls in their care and the families who choose their nurseries.

I advocate that whoever is caring for a young child, especially a boy, should provide:

Continuity of
Individual
Love
Learning and
Attention

CILLA for short.

Be careful how you interpret the learning section of this acronym. I am certainly not suggesting structured learning or a formalized curriculum. I am advocating learning from role models, from caring relationships, from fun, from hugs and kisses. I am advocating learning from a carer who knows that babbling 'buh buh' means that the child is ripe for having Baa Baa black sheep sung (Manolson et al.) *every time* the nappy is changed. The toddler who likes hissing like a snake is ready for 'What goes in your socks Sam' (Out of the Ark) and all the lovely actions that go with it and the boy who wants to kick needs taking outside to kick leaves or splash in puddles rather than being told that he is naughty and kicking is bad.

When considering the provision a nursery or childcare setting offers, especially for boys, ask yourself the following questions:

- Does the nursery offer your boy a key person who he can relate to as the 'mummy-shaped carer'? Is this person with him all or most of the time?
- Do the nursery staff understand the needs of boys and most importantly have a *positive attitude* towards them?
- Are the staff in the nursery encouraged and supported to use appropriate physical contact with the babies and toddlers?
- Are songs and music an important part of every day?
- Are babies held and rocked as songs are sung?
- Is nappy time treated as an opportunity for eye contact, smiles, raspberries on the belly, silly songs . . . 'mummy-shaped stuff'?
- Do the ratios allow staff sufficient time to really know and care about your boy?
- Does the nursery encourage the staff to share their passions with the children?
- Does the nursery have sufficient space to allow your boy to move around as he needs to?
- Does your nursery have an outside area and encourage gross motor skills *before* fine are expected of them?
- Are parents and grandparents welcome at the nursery?
- Is there flexibility in the sessions and timing to meet the needs of the boy and his parents?
- Can parents eat with the children if they wish?
- Is food and drink freshly prepared with no artificial additives (HACSG)?
- Do the staff use *positive* language and avoid labelling the child by his behaviour?
- Do the nursery stick rigidly to their routines or is there some flexibility for individuals' needs and individualized learning?
- Are the children encouraged to spend time in mixed age groups?
- Within reason, are the children allowed to simply 'be'?
- Are screen activities limited?
- Are the boys allowed to explore and get dirty?
- Do the early years professionals love the children and love their jobs?

Parents are being encouraged to put their children into toddler groups, nursery schools and reception classes earlier and earlier. Certainly by the age of three, most boys are ready to have some time with other children and access to a whole range of vibrant, stimulating activities through play. What many of them are not yet ready for is being away from mum for whole days, in fact whole weeks. Flexibility is needed to match the needs of the child and the needs of the parents.

In *Raising Boys* Biddulph explains that boys really need their mummies from birth to six years old. This goes back when our ancestors lived in the wild. Up to the age of six, boys would be in a communal living space with other children and, most of the time, with women. The younger children learned from the older ones and the older ones learned to be kind, caring and understand the responsibilities of having younger children around. (Look out for nurseries and children's centres that realize the importance of this and be wary of 'baby rooms'.) Boys need and have very close attachments to their mummies in these years and foundation stage professionals need to be acutely aware of this.

The importance of comfort

An observation I have made is that many mothers treat their young sons as 'little men'. They expect them to be tough, they tell them not to cry when they are hurt and some, usually lone mothers who have experienced hurt, sadly flag up the inherited traits so disliked in their fathers. We need to remember that every boy is an individual with a right to grow up to be judged on his own merits, not those despised in his father or those perpetuated by labels and stereotyping. Even the most caring mothers often brush aside boys' upsets or injuries. Boys do suffer more accidents than girls so mothers of sons are more familiar with scabs, plaster casts and Accident and Emergency.

Kagan says, 'Because androgens (male hormones) have a calming effect on the nerve cells in the amygdala (a brain structure linked with a person's mental and emotional state) boys show less fear.'

Boys may show less fear but they still need to be comforted when they are distressed. Sunderland stresses the importance of boys experiencing being comforted to enable them to be empathetic and caring towards others as well as for positive mental health. 'Fear, anger and sadness activate the lower brain (this functions with more basic responses) ... children need *help* to calm down and develop pathways to control these.'

Risk taking

The flip side of comforting and perhaps protecting boys is another reason for boys of 0–6 having a good man in their life. They need to be allowed to take risks.

'Risk and comfort both tend to grow into a habit – you get used to both of them' (Ortberg). For a boy to grow into a well-balanced man he needs to have experienced risk and comfort and he needs to know when each one is appropriate.

Biddulph advocates learning many lessons about how to become a good man through rough games with dad, a bitter-sweet balance of risk and comfort with a whole bunch of adrenalin and fun thrown in. The judgement of dad or a trusted man can be beneficial in other areas too, some as simple as how high a boy should be allowed to climb up a tree.

It takes a confident mum, especially with a first boy, or a boy following girls to be at ease with the fact that boys do take risks; they need to take risks to learn what their growing bodies can do. You wouldn't upgrade from a Ford Fiesta to a Porsche and still drive it the same way. You need to test it out. Boys know they want to test it, mums need to ensure they are in a reasonably safe environment in order to do it.

Next time you go to a play park watch the mothers of boys. Those darting beneath the play frame to catch their precious offspring in case they fall are at the beginning of their journey into being the mother of boys. Those joining in or sitting calmly on a bench casting an occasional eye have passed through the initiation ceremony and are probably the mother of one older boy, or maybe two or three. Boys in schools and nurseries need to be able to take risks and to be comforted. They need to be allowed to be boys.

Although mums are so important, a dad's role with young boys is fundamental. Apart from being a rational eye for risk taking, one story of a boy brought up solely by mum shows us how there are things that only a male knows best. A five-year-old boy had a day with his uncle. During the day they went to a toilet and the boy, after he had finished his wee, reached for toilet paper to wipe himself. The uncle gently but firmly explained to him that this is not something that big boys and men would do. He probably saved that boy from considerable teasing in later life. This is a pretty obvious example but how many subtleties are there about how to be a good man that as a woman I have no idea of, and probably never will.

At a later stage in their lives, if a man was raising a daughter alone I'm confident he would seek the advice of a trusted woman to prepare his daughter for menstruation. It would take a bold mother to invite a man, however well trusted, to prepare her son for how to deal with masturbation. It is a surprise to me that I found it difficult to write that word let alone presume to discuss the subject, even in a factual, dos and don't manner with my sons. I do thank God for my wonderful husband every day and for so many good men in my boys' lives.

Back in schools and nurseries, early years professionals *of both sexes must* be allowed to hug and cuddle boys. They must work alongside mums and dads understanding the needs of these young families. They need to have time to really know these boys and to understand them without forcing children to jump through hoops that are at odds with their needs. They need to have fun, friendship and laughter. Parents and teachers need to ensure that, at whatever age boys begin their education it is a wonderful positive experience. I question whether we allow children simply to experience childhood, do we allow boys to be boys?

Points for Action – Zero to Six

Delight in your boys, touch, smile, rock, laugh, enjoy, indulge and tell everyone how wonderful they are.

Remember boys need their mums most between 0 and 6, especially when they have to go to nursery or to school.

Choose childcare that ticks all your boxes and fills the 'mummy-shaped gap'.

Observe a trusted man playing with your boy to see how far his risk taking should go.

Remember he is still a boy not a man; he needs to be treated as a child and to know how it feels to be comforted.

Six to fourteen years – great dad wanted

I firmly believe that there are many more good men in our society than bad ones, in spite of what the media would have us believe. If you are in doubt ask yourself 'How many times have I walked past a man and he *hasn't* mugged me?'

Our mission is to get these good men involved in the lives of growing men. Although boys from zero to six need fathers, they are drawn towards their mothers, from six up to fourteen their focus begins to change. In an ideal world they *need* their dad, a constant, active, loving dad. From six to fourteen dads are crucial. They are powerful role models and need to be aware of how potently their words, actions and emotions transmit to their sons.

In an ideal world a father is the biggest influence on a boy in these middle years. When men were hunters, thousands of years ago, it was most likely that, as soon as a boy was strong enough he would leave the communal home group and begin to learn about being male and what it means to be a man.

There are some close links with his rate of development here. It is no coincidence that by the age of seven the boy would likely have all his cranial-caudal, proximal-distal connections in place so he would no longer have the clumsiness of so many young boys. His nerve endings would have finally reached his fingertips so he would be able to begin some fine motor tasks especially tool making. His brain connections are more likely to enable him to be still and quiet, be patient while waiting for the prey or catching fish. His body would be strong and he would be emotionally stable from the time he has spent allowing him to develop at his own pace in the family unit. He would understand social skills and understand the need to take his place with the older boys and men on the hunt. He would have been allowed freedom to explore and would have learnt from the risks he had taken. He would be well armed and ready to venture out into the great outdoors with the men.

> His nerve endings would have finally reached his fingertips.

It seems to me that the list of skills that this boy has developed by the age of seven in order to be apprenticed to hunt with his father would stand him in good stead for learning today, in our schools and families in the twenty-first century.

This boy would now spend less time learning from women; he needs to learn how to function as a young man in a group of males. This is such a crucial skill and unless they are in a football team (beware, that does have its own dangers) many boys spend more time bonding with plasma than with peer groups or people.

If a boy is not able to spend time with his dad then he may suffer from something that has been described as 'father hunger' (Biddulph 1994). He may then seek out alternative ways to get the things he would otherwise be getting from a good father.

> Boys spend more time bonding with plasma than with peer groups or people.

Emotions and how to handle them are a big issue for fathers and good male role models. Boys are often scared of their powerful emotions and need to see how adult males deal with anger, rage, sadness and challenge in appropriate ways to move from the historical role of man as hunter into a more balanced outlook for the twenty-first century. They need to see that words are more powerful than fists and they can only learn this through positive examples.

Transition

In this age group boys often struggle with the transition from junior school to secondary education. It is crucial that we get this right and that boys feel empowered and supported through this change. It is the time in education where the largest proportion of boys stumble and many never regain their footing.

Mums can play a really valuable role but it is only a male who knows first hand about the testosterone-fuelled dynamics of a secondary school corridor, sports team or boys' toilet. We need to plan ahead for transition among schools and find a way of getting continuity, ideally for all but certainly for the most vulnerable (Chapter 11). Dads can make a huge difference by being accessible, open, honest yet respectful. They can also make a huge difference by their absence. If there is no father or father figure in a young boy's life then he is like a ship with big sails and no rudder. Trusted family friends, Godparents, relatives can all make a big difference in these situations but choose your role models well and treat them well. They play such a crucial part in your son's life.

> If there is no father or father figure in a young boy's life then he is like a ship with big sails and no rudder.

Many absent fathers are not absent from the home at all . . . but their positive input and influence is absent. Being a great dad is not a part-time role. Dads have to wear the T-shirt every minute and be prepared to be there alongside their boy's mother even if they have differences of opinion or if they are on a phone link at the other side of the planet. It is a father's role to teach their boy how to respect his mother and how to relate respectfully to women in general.

There is a problem that occurs for many women as boys grow, past six years, into the stage where they would not have, historically, taken instruction from females. It also coincides with the boy being too big to be carried by his mother. She can no longer 'make him' do as she asks.

Boys may unconsciously dismiss what women say, shirk from doing what their mother or female teacher asks. Dads need to show that they have respect for their child's teacher, and even if they have fallen out, dads need to speak respectfully about and to their son's mother. They need to be seen to appreciate her, value her and treat her with respect. This is so important as our boys need to know how to treat a woman well to ensure their own happy future families.

So often children in fragmented families are caught up as pawns in the bitter game of chess between separated partners. This is simply not fair. In or out of relationships parents need to remember to sort out their differences respectfully away from the children. If they disagree around the children then they must resolve these differences with calm negotiation and respectful conflict resolution. Boys especially need to learn how to deal with conflict appropriately and learn that it is a *strength* to seek help when it is needed.

We know that we don't live in a perfect world but if we are alert to some of the challenges facing boys between the ages of seven and fourteen we may be able to support the very people who are best placed to make things better for our boys.

Big Issues for Raising Boys Aged 6–14

- Boys need good constant male role models, especially good dads.
- In 1999 'Most parents and children – but fathers in particular – viewed providing an income for the family as the central part of fathering' (Joseph Rowntree Foundation Fathers Work and Family Life Report). This is changing but very slowly.
- Many boys relate more with celebrities and sports stars than their dads. They follow these as role models whether good or bad.
- Dads need to understand just how important their role is with young boys (and girls).
- Lone mothers and concerned parents understandably often over-protect their boys. Boys need more opportunities to learn how to be good men at first hand.
- Boys spend most of their waking lives in schools. There are simply not enough good male role models in our schools.
- With the advent of extended services, boys have the opportunity to spend even more of their waking hours in school. We need to seize this opportunity and use all the potential it has to offer to get dads and good male role models involved.
- The majority of men that boys see in schools are either headteachers or caretakers. Men (and women) who are passionate about a positive future for boys must have a higher profile in everyday school life.
- Boys don't associate dads and men with learning or reading. Boys need to know that reading is 'cool' and see their dads actively demonstrating these skills as their most powerful role models.
- Many more boys than girls have ADHD or similar 'disorders'. Many of these 'disorders' can run in families. Dads, remaining undiagnosed, do not have the strategies or knowledge of how to overcome the challenges of ADHD as adults or how to help their sons (HACSG).

- Boys between the ages of six and fourteen go through many physical and emotional changes. They are less likely than girls to ask for help to understand these and how to deal with them practically and emotionally.
- Boys often lack a constant relationship with a man they can trust and turn to.
- Many female teachers of boys aged seven to fourteen struggle to understand them and to gain their respect. They need support and training as to the reasons boys of this age may be behaving in this way.
- Many mothers of boys aged six to fourteen struggle to gain their respect, especially if there is another male the boy may need to impress. Boys need a good male role model to teach them how to respect women.
- Boys of this age are often feared in our communities. We need to make opportunities for community members to know the good in boys and build positive relationships.
- Television programmes for six and over rarely offer positive role models. We need to promote discerning viewing and help change the types of programmes that are offered.
- Boys of this age are often labelled as a breed. Labels cause real damage to those who are branded by them. We need to break this culture.
- Boys over ten can get a criminal record. This is far too young and shows the shallow understanding our society has of how boys behave and what they need to help them grow in positive ways.
- Many boys are simply lost, as are many of the women who struggle to bring them up.
- Dads need help to be able to talk to boys about emotions. Factual support comes much more easily. Boys with absent fathers struggle to find this support (FNF, parents UK, fathers direct).
- Dads are rarely seen in schools and many feel school is the domain of women. Dads need to be welcome and seen as key players in all schools and nurseries especially from six years up.
- When many fathers see their sons it is for such a small proportion of their time that they feel it is important to show the boys who is in charge. They often use harsh, dominant methods to let the boy know who is in charge. A firm approach also needs to be warm (Palmer) or the boy will lack self-esteem and easily go off the rails.
- Dads often have rigid work schedules. Flexi time for all parents with children under eighteen (or over if they have special needs) needs to be an everyday expectation *including those parents who are in the teaching profession.*
- Many absent fathers and 'weekend dads' buy 'stuff' for their children to show they care. Love does not equal stuff. This well-meaning generosity also causes real problems for the mother as it undermines the often mundane consistency that she needs to maintain during the week.
- Girls learn how to dress and behave appropriately from being with mums, other girls and talking about these issues. Boys with absent dads have little guidance in this and do not talk about these issues in the same way.
- Boys need to learn to function as positive members of teams, especially male teams. Dads need to guide them towards the best sort of teams, away from the worst and support boys who find being a team player a challenge and therefore may find it hard to fit in.
- Boys with no positive role model gravitate towards styles that they see in the media and inappropriate role models. This leaves them open to being judged by their appearance and often misinterpreted.

(Continued)

Growing good men fourteen plus-respect

'Young people today have no respect.'

If you have managed to go through life without hearing this you have done well. Respect is an important issue, for young and old alike. The older generation often find it difficult to understand the changes in how young people are being brought up but the 'Respect Agenda' has rightly become a much bigger issue. There is now an actual document targeted at increasing respect in our communities.

It carries some powerful statements:

- 'The only person who can start the cycle of respect is you.'
- 'Give respect get respect.'
- 'The foundation of our future is our young.'
- The future depends on unlocking the *positive* potential of young people.

I consider the last of these statements to be the most pertinent. When we consider the future of boys we have talked at length about the damage that society, stresses of the twenty-first century and the media is causing. We have looked at the stereotypical view with which many people view boys. We have looked at the crucial role of good, constant, understanding mums and dads. What more can there be?

From the age of fourteen, both historically and in other cultures across the world, boys are treated like men. They are expected to have more adult responsibilities and certainly expect to be treated more like young men than children. They are less likely to take advice or guidance from their parents!

Gangs

Back in the times of the hunter, boys at this age would be given a rite of initiation and accepted into the pack of hunters as one of the men. They would learn from the other men, a kind of early apprenticeship and soon be one of the 'gang'. We see this need for approval and being part of a group outside the family with boys gravitating towards street gangs and groups that offer them a sense of identity. These gangs can be lawless, offer no older male guidance and restraint, therefore we see behaviours that are not of men, but of boys without men. Is this the identity we want them to have?

> Boys gravitate towards street gangs and groups that offer them a sense of identity.

I found it fascinating to discover what happened to a group of adolescent bull elephants (McBride Dabbs et al.). They usually live in mixed-aged family groups but due to a cull of old bulls, the behaviour of the young elephants changed. They no longer had the elders to supervise them. These young elephants got into trouble. They began to kill white rhinos, another endangered species, apparently for sport. Their testosterone levels had risen considerably earlier than they would normally have and they had stayed high for as long as three months rather than the normal few days. Kruger, the national park where this happened now relocates elephants in family groups rather than culling the elders.

Have we caused some of the problems for teenaged boys and society by effectively denying them access to elders? It is a disturbing thought . . .

If as parents and teachers we want boys to have good role models we need to involve *positive* role models in the lives of boys. We need society to *believe* in boys but most importantly we need boys to *believe* in themselves.

'Belief is very powerful and we need to align it and make sure our beliefs about ourselves are good, positive and helpful in our lives' (Sieger).

Special People

Boys need to be surrounded by chosen people, trusted to offer advice, friendships and guidance. These will be powerful people in the lives of growing men.

Parents of teenagers need to step back (just a little) and trust the people they have chosen to be there for their boys. Nigella Lawson, celebrity chef and parent, says that when people become parents they are no longer the picture, they become the frame. When boys hit fourteen I suggest that they break out of their parents' frame and look for a bigger, different frame to shape the picture of their future lives as young men today.

As parents, my husband and I were well aware of the vital role these special people would have in our sons' lives. We were lucky to have trusted friends willing to be generous and active in the lives of our boys. We chose people who had similar values to ourselves, who we enjoyed having in our lives, but also we chose people with a *passion*. It did not matter (within reason) what the passion was but we figured that if these people had a passion for something they would be well placed to help our sons find their own passions and support them in achieving them.

> We chose people with a passion!

Derek is special to my youngest son and his passion is rescuing bats from old ladies' lofts! Whenever they spend time together there is always a story to be shared or an injured bat to feed. My son adores his Godfather and benefits so much from the relationship. I have a sneaky suspicion that it works both ways and the 'Batman' rather enjoys the relationship too.

We need to find ways to help families who do not have obvious respected role models to find good, willing men to make a difference to the futures of their boys.

If a child's special people happen to be Godparents these have traditionally been chosen with a bias towards the gender of the child. This is not crucial but the two to one balance does seem to be a positive ratio for boys. Wouldn't it be great if boys had the opportunity throughout school for two out of three of their teachers, youth leaders or teaching assistants to be men? Whilst I do not advocate devaluing all the great work that understanding female teachers do for our boys, I do believe we have scope to greatly increase the numbers of men in education and to consider some single-sex groups, both for study and importantly for pastoral and life skills. Homing in on peoples' passions is a key to this whether they are male or female.

Thomas Dee in 'The Why Chromosome' in the *Education Next Journal* states that 'simply put, girls have better educational opportunities when taught by women and boys are better off when taught by men'. Although single sex schools certainly benefit from the opportunity to specialize in one gender I firmly believe that boys need to learn to live, communicate with and co-operate with girls as equal partners. The best school can blend mixed-sex and single-sex groupings to gain fabulous results as well as the human skills our future men so badly need.

Achieving good results is always a thorny issue with the gap still widening between boys' and girls' achievement and being reported, therefore making boys feel even worse than they already do.

> 'A study of 25000 pupils by Stanford University economist Thomas Dee found children did 4% better in tests when their teachers were of the same sex' (BBC News, 29 August 2006).

'We also have a culture that boys buy into, a perception that doing well at school is "girly"' (Alan Johnson, MP as Education Secretary, 15 March 2007). 'With only 31% of university applications being from boys and a lack of trades available to train up less academic pupils we need to make a difference and we need to make it now.'

In order to have a happy, successful adult life it is more than desirable that a young man likes the job or profession he is going to follow. In order to do this he needs someone, in or out of school, to help him find what he is good at, to help him find what is important to him, to help him find his *passion*. If someone is able to work at something for which they have a passion they are much more likely to do a good job, to have staying power, to persevere when the going gets tough, in short, be willing and successful workers. Surely with so much competition these are attributes we need to promote in the workforce of the future. Finding each boy's passion and having a good male role model are paramount.

> 'Doing well at school is "girly."'

Schools, particularly now that they have a raised community profile, have to take a lead in this, as for many families finding a good male role model to give of their time and themselves for their son is a tall order. Now that businesses are being encouraged to have social responsibility policies, there is a real hope that more good men will be able to be released from work in order to support these boys. Schools need to be proactive; they need to broker these links and nurture them. They need to offer a safe place and time for mentor and young man to get together.

Girls talk about periods, boys, sex, spots, hairstyles, whatever is a big issue for them as they journey through their adolescent years. Boys are in danger of journeying alone and joining the wrong band-wagon if it happens to be the only one he can find. David Leggett who supports young people and their families through his work in youth justice finds that often there is not a man to be seen and states, 'That's just the way it is'.

Boys are in danger of journeying alone.

If a teenage boy finds solace in a gang he is likely to dress in a similar way to that gang to fit in. Sad but true, your whole demeanour changes according to what you are wearing. It is almost as if these boys are donning labels for themselves and society is all too quick to read them.

This can be a self-fulfilling prophecy. No one is likely to make eye contact, smile and certainly not touch a young man if his clothes are giving out messages that spell DANGER. He is likely to be avoided and ignored by all but his gang.

'To be ignored is not only unpleasant, it is also, from an evolutionary perspective, unsafe' (de Botton).

These boys are likely to receive their only attention from their gang or negative attention from their community and the police. They are unlikely to receive positive attention let alone affection which they still so desperately need. As Dr Kraemer of the Tavistock Clinic says 'a lack of affection could result in . . . depression and suicide.'

If a boy has low self-esteem and is depressed it shows in his body language. It is this very body language that bullies and criminals observe to choose their victims. Their body language spells out their vulnerability. It seems that unless our boys get good role models they are in danger from all angles.

Teenage boys are in crisis!

Initiation ceremonies

Many boys moving into their teenage years are left with little support. They have to draw on their own devices. Girls tend to fare rather better. They are rarely left without support for those challenging years of growing from a girl into a woman. She has a natural initiation ceremony; the buying of the bra, the first period are all taken care of by a supportive 'sisterhood'.

I was delighted to hear from Tim, a caring father of girls that, when his daughters began their periods, he considered his role seriously. He took each one out, just father and daughter. They chose a beautiful ring and went for a special meal out together. They talked of the responsibilities of growing as a woman and the anticipation of the responsibilities and delights to come. Tim spoke of his pride and his support for his young woman in her future. How must this have made his daughter feel?

How wonderful it would be if each adolescent boy could have his 'moving into manhood' marked with such respect and love. Maybe dad or a father figure could take the boy away for a weekend, to do outdoor stuff together.

> Talking always happens better for guys if they are doing 'stuff'.

Maybe they could complete a challenge together. They may include some other respected men for part of the time but the one to one is important. Perhaps companies that sell razors might offer 'Outward Bound' packages as a special 'Moving into Manhood' pack.

I am not a man. I can never know what would best mark this event for an individual young man. Maybe it is along the lines of community work or even National Service as used to exist and still does in some countries. What I ask is, if you have responsibility for a young man who is obviously 'learning to drive a man's body' please find a way to help him mark this momentous change with a trusted, caring and respected man. Find ways to teach him to positively work with the risks and responsibilities his future holds, to believe in himself and his future knowing that you believe in him.

Points for Action – Growing Good Men Fourteen Plus

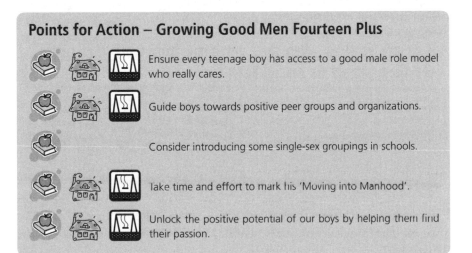

Ensure every teenage boy has access to a good male role model who really cares.

Guide boys towards positive peer groups and organizations.

Consider introducing some single-sex groupings in schools.

Take time and effort to mark his 'Moving into Manhood'.

Unlock the positive potential of our boys by helping them find their passion.

10 Caring contact and communication

British parents cite coping with today's long hours' culture and seeing enough of their children as their number one stress.

How can a parent manage a child with an ASBO if the parent is never there?

Many parents are too busy to give their parents a routine so important to a child's stability.

A male nursery nurse left the profession after being reprimanded for allowing a three-year-old to hold his hand.

Teachers are scared to touch children in case they are sued.

If parents and children are only ever together when they are tired and hungry how can they ever see the best in each other?

A strong father–child relationship has been found to help children do better in adult life.

Parents today have less time for bedtime stories and other activities that involve close physical contact with their children

People today are too busy to b~ families

People rarely find time to laugh, to smile, to relax

Boys who spend time and feel on par with their fathers are more popular with their peers and show less aggression in the playground

Hugging is a basic need – it changes your internal environment.

Dads are so tired when they get home from work that boys see them simply as disciplinarians

Research indicates that a parent's physical attention helps the stress system in the infant's brain develop and function normally

When dads are actively involved in family life and in school it has a positive effect on their exam results

Memories are made of this

I would like to try something. Find a quiet place. Close your eyes and take yourself back to when you were a child. I would like you to recall a positive experience from your childhood where being with a particular adult made you feel good. Take time and remember everything about it. Where were you, what could you hear? Were you warm or cold? What could you smell or taste? What could you see or feel? Take time and savour the memory.

How do you feel when you recall that experience?

Were you alone with the person or with someone else you cared about?

Were you close to that person either emotionally or physically?

Did you trust them and feel you could confide in them?

Were you able to recapture those emotions, the way it made you feel?

I truly hope that each of you reading this was able to recapture a wonderful moment with someone special to you.

Were you surprised by the amount of detail you remembered, the different senses that were engaged? This is what real experiences are made of. The experiences that make a difference to the emotions, to the way a person grows, to the 'internal environment.'

I would like to consider now, how often you have the opportunity to share such experiences with the boys you teach or care about.

When I reflected on this I felt sad. I did not take enough time with each of my boys (and it is so important that as parents we *make* time for each child as an individual). I had got into the spiral of doing too many things, prioritizing those things that other people demanded, simply being *too* busy.

> Make time for what matters.

This has become an epidemic in our culture with teachers suffering a very similar fate to parents and carers. We all need to decide what really matters and make time for the things and the people that deserve the best of us.

Touch

In families, girls are more likely to gain the attention and time they need. (We need to look out for those who don't.) They ask questions, they talk, they tell their parents how terrible or wonderful their day has been without them having to ask.

Girls are also more likely to gain that vital human interaction, appropriate physical touch.

Experiences that engage our senses are the most powerful, the most memorable. Touch is often the sense that gets missed out, especially as boys get older.

'The skin is the largest sense organ and scientists have found that positive touching subdues the "fight or flight" response, relaxing blood pressure, the digestive system, body temperature, muscles and heart rate' (de Botton).

Girls touch each other much more than boys; girls groom each other, sometimes they find it hard to stop. I remember when I was teaching there would always be a girl rearranging another girl's ponytail. It is partly because of hair that girls demand more physical contact from their parents and from each other. It is a rare parent who will let their daughter leave the house without spending time 'doing' her hair. Girls paint each other's nails and experiment with make-up. All of these include appropriate physical touch and usually a lot of conversation and problem solving and emotions along the way.

Boys in Western society usually have short hair. Many boys, including mine, often leave the house without having had any grooming from their parents. Some sadly leave without any attention from their parents. Boys generally take longer to get organized for school in the morning, causing more tension and leaving less time for parents to give nurturing touch to set them up for the day. It is much more likely that they will be berated for having forgotten their reading book and have their shirt tucked in rather briskly.

In a children's home in Hamburg the children really benefit from a ten-minute back and shoulder rub from a female member of staff just before they go to bed.

'We have no problem with physical contact with the children. Some have had such negative experiences, we need to help them learn to trust again, and this includes being touched by another person' (Marie Nemitz, care worker).

For many reasons boys typically receive far less tender human touch than girls and the amount of *caring* physical contact from dads after they pass the 'pick 'em up and hug 'em' stage is negligible. (Steve Biddulph's (1998) rough games with Dad can really help bridge the gap here.)

> Boys typically receive far less tender human touch than girls.

Time to talk

At the end of a long day, when a junior school boy is asked 'What did you do at school today?' the response is universal.

'Nuffink.'

On my workshop it was almost unbelievable how many parents had heard this same reply, day in and day out. I have taught in primary schools for years and nowhere had I seen 'Nuffink' prescribed.

Joking aside, a boy is tired, stressed and hungry after school, three good reasons why his testosterone and blood sugar levels are not conducive to talking and probably not to listening either. He needs to rectify all three conditions before any constructive communication can take place.

If this boy is in an after-school club, with an au pair, a nanny or is home alone when he needs a trusted person to help him solve his problem, he may gravitate to the age old male pattern of bottling it up. The danger of constantly bottling up one's worries is that, like a bottle of fizzy drink – when shaken it may explode. If his parent is there and too tied up, busy, tired or stressed to listen then the boy and his concerns may never be heard; the boy may learn that it is better not to speak his concerns. Emotional literacy, circle time and good, caring communication are crucial skills if boys are going to become successful men in a world where men and women are expected to be equal partners.

> The danger of constantly bottling up one's worries is that, like a bottle of fizzy drink when shaken it may explode.

Whatever his age, if a boy is never heard, what chance has he of being understood and respected, let alone nurtured and enjoyed?

Surviving, striving, thriving

In my Positive Power workshop I use the diagram in Figure 10.1 focus on the power of touch and tender human contact.

The width of the heart at each point represents the amount of contact we have with each of the boys we care about. A large part of this is overcoming the stigma, the stiff upper lip and the fear some people have of physical touch, however appropriate.

> If someone we respect touches us it shows they approve of us.

Hugs at home are certainly appropriate but how often do we as teachers rub the shoulder of a boy we have in our class, especially if we have had some

Thriving

Striving

Surviving

challenging times. How often do we sit and share lunch with him or have him take a walk with us (Daly)? How often do we pay him a complement, talk to him gently or give him warm eye contact? The schools who know the power of this contact, this touch, reap the rewards.

Thomas, an eleven-year-old said that when his form tutor touched him on the shoulder it made him feel strong . . . 'I know he believes I can do it'.

I believe that all schools from nurseries to sixth form should have a 'Caring Contact and Communication Policy' or APT Policy (Appropriate Physical Touch) that they share and agree with the children, parents and teachers. The relationships teachers have with their boys and girls, between the children and between all the adults in the school community are so much more caring, more positive than those that have a 'no touch' policy or with no policy at all. It also makes a world of difference to the thorny issue of bullying.

Surviving

The families and schools where boys are simply 'surviving' would benefit from reflecting how much time and commitment is given to caring, contact and communication. They would be represented at the bottom of the heart diagram. As more time, touch and contact is present then the boys begin to make progress, relationships improve as does health, self-esteem, confidence . . . the list goes on. Many relationships that fall into this category have fallen into a pattern, a rut. The adults have often come to rely on the patterns that are there and work 'well enough'. They don't see that there needs to be much more engagement and vitality between them and the boy.

If a parent is struggling with how to make this contact then I recommend referring back to that memorable experience, the way it engaged so many memories through senses. Doing things with our hands, especially mucky ones, outdoor activities where we can feel the breeze on our skin, hear the wind in the trees, huddling together around a warm campfire or freezing in a tent and, again anything involving food are so powerful to help us connect, share experiences in a caring way.

Teachers need to invigorate their sessions with KAVES (Chapter 7) and vibrant learning styles, not forgetting that vital ingredient – fun! What will help the boys to remember this experience?

> How can I help the subject to connect with these boys and what they care about (Daly)?

Striving

Parents or educators, many of us are in the middle of the heart. We are striving and so are the boys in our care. We are doing some of what we need to but we could do more. What we need to know is that we are working our way towards the relationship at the top of the heart. If we are stuck in the middle or even slipping down, then we need to stop, reassess and see what we can do to reinvigorate our relationship, our teaching, our school, our family life. Do not be afraid to ask for help. Someone else, looking at our situation with different eyes can really revitalize and refresh.

Thriving

At the top of the heart where time, touch, caring, communication and contact are priorities the children and their relationships are thriving. Adults and children in schools, families or communities can relax, learn and grow together. They can have fun, and, as the heart represents, have the strength to overcome the ups and downs of life together. Adults and children benefit immensely and everyone deserves relationships based on respect and trust.

When my colleagues and I go into schools to visit student teachers we get a feeling in the first few moments that says so much about that school environment, about its relationships and how happy and secure the children and adults feel. You get a similar feeling when you walk into some people's homes.

In families and, in a different way in schools, you can almost feel the love, the care, the warm feeling that builds the positive brain connections that equip our boys and the people who care about them for such a positive future.

Points for Action – Caring Contact and Communication

Make time for what matters especially great communication.

At home, make time for each boy as an individual.

At school, make time to *know* each boy as an individual.

Build relationships based on respect and trust.

Find ways to use more 'Caring contact' and 'Appropriate Physical Touch'.

Part 3
Man as Hunter to Man as Mentor in Schools, Families and Communities

Respect, understanding and relationships **11**

Schools, families and communities have a responsibility to get it right for boys and to do that the starting point has to be good, respectful relationships, not just with boys but with everyone who has a part in their lives.

> We have a responsibility to get it right for boys and to do that the starting point has to be good, respectful relationships.

Most men and many boys know about Pre Menstrual Tension and the reasons behind it. They are accommodating and understanding of the women in their lives when they experience PMT. Do women have a similar depth of understanding when boys and men demonstrate behaviours that have been engrained in their make-up for centuries? Do boys and men understand why they feel and behave as they do in certain situations?

The legacy of testosterone

We are all different and must always hold on to this, but if we learn a little more of how testosterone affected our ancestors it can help us to understand each other so much better, enabling us as adults to be the stable roots and fertile soil from which to grow great boys.

We know from Testosterone Triggers (Chapter 6) that the effects of testosterone on the developing brain and body are very powerful in sculpting each boy for the man he is to become. There are many theories that testosterone gears up boys to be equipped to be hunters, after all, until the industrial revolution brought us factories and many different jobs, it was necessary for men to find food for his family whether through farming or originally through hunting. We also know that hunting is not top of the list for what successful men need to do in the twenty-first century but do we know the legacy that thousands of years of hunting skills have left for our boys?

I do not presume to suggest that any one boy would necessarily fit the stereotype of man as hunter. I would however ask you to reflect on the links we are about to make. Consider if any of these match with your behaviours or those of the boys and men in your lives. If the answer is 'yes' how can we use this understanding to make our living, learning, working and playing together less stressful, more respectful and more cohesive?

Man as hunter

There is debate about how long man has been functioning on earth. We know it is at least 50,000 years. It is certainly longer that man has been expected to function as a hunter than it is that Western society has been expecting men and women to become multi-tasking, multi-functioning beings, to cross over from traditional roles. Men are now expected to be all things to all people, especially in families. They are expected to demonstrate emotional intelligence and organizational skills never before in their blueprint. In these early days of a new era of gender expectations . . . a little understanding can go a long way.

The 'Man as Hunter' theory is far from rocket science. It is simply a way of understanding some of the ways that men and women typically function based on the premise that:

- Women lived communally in a cave, camp or hearth with all the children of six and under.
- Boys from the age of six or seven would join the men when they went on hunting expeditions while girls continued to live with the women.
- At the age of fourteen boys would pass through some kind of 'rite of initiation' and become one of the hunters in their own right.

Of course this is far from what happens today with all the different pressures, professions and pleasures of twenty-first-century living; however, we no longer eat grass but nature still endows us with an appendix!

Subscribe to the 'Man as Hunter' theory as much or as little as you like but take the time to see how the theory matches up with the strengths of boys highlighted earlier (Chapter 2). Perhaps we can learn a little to help all relationships run a little smoother.

Karon did just this. She spent a morning on the workshop learning about 'Testosterone Triggers' and 'Man as Hunter'. She left the workshop early at lunchtime looking anxious. I was concerned and later was happy to see that she had returned for the afternoon session. When, in a quiet moment, I asked her how things were she explained: She had called her husband to apologize for how she had misunderstood him. The previous evening Karon had insisted on telling him her news even though he had tried, unsuccessfully, to explain that this was a difficult time for him to listen.

Several months later Karon contacted me. She wanted to let me know what a difference the knowledge and understanding she had gained from the workshop had made . . . to the boys she cared for as a teaching assistant, to the relationship with her son and . . . to her relationship with her husband!

What are the aims of hunting? To find food, to compete and have a forum to show who is stronger, who has the best skills. It is also a forum to prove your worth in the group and to bring home the biggest trophy in order to impress the most desirable mate back at the communal hearth. Let us see how this matches up with some of the male behaviours we see today.

Physical activity

More than simply sport

So many of the sports men excel at have much in common with hunting. In many sports men work together towards a common goal, as if hunting prey. Men are good at working together if there is a shared target but even within that team work there is competition. Women working together are more inclined to comply, to be flexible to each other's needs as they would when working together in the communal hearth. The 'need to compete' in males is almost innate. Asking for help is simply not an option. It is important for each hunter to be the best hunter he can be, and be seen to be so.

The responsibility this places on sports coaches working today is vast. They have the power to make or break a boy's self-esteem and confidence by the way they speak to their charges in front of their peers. David Hemery has many really useful suggestions for coaches, teachers and parents alike in *How to Help Your Child to Find the Champion within Themselves*.

Sport should always be a positive forum for praise. (See SPADE Chapter 2.) Any criticism where peers or siblings are within earshot should be given quietly, discretely and respectfully helping a boy to take the criticism and then feel supported with achievable steps back up the ladder of success and self-esteem. Ortberg offers much useful guidance on how to handle failure constructively in the book *If You Want to Walk on Water You've Got to Get Out of the Boat*.

So many boys to whom sport does not come easily are humiliated, demoralized and destroyed by the comments of their coaches, teachers and often vociferous dads in front of their peers. This then gives a licence to the other boys to treat this boy as a victim in the very same way. Many schools, groups and families where boys are victims of bullying could benefit from reflecting on how the adults communicate, both with words and with their all-powerful body language.

Teams

Boys would naturally seek out teams to belong to as they would have joined the hunting group at fourteen. Parents and teachers need to be proactive in helping boys find appropriate teams to join, and schools need to ensure boys have access to good role models of older boys to help guide boys, especially those around fourteen, to strong, supportive, positive groups.

Boys just need to move

As we discovered in Chapter 7, boys just need to move. They occupy more physical space than girls (another reason for smaller class sizes) do and they have surges of physical energy. They have times when their body simply needs to move and they find it nigh on impossible to concentrate on anything else. This is a large factor of why sitting still in class for long periods is so difficult for boys. Kinaesthetic learning, while it does not suit all, is helpful for so many of our boys.

If you notice that a boy keeps repeating an action it is most likely that his body needs to do this before he can move on the next stage of development. (This often happens with rocking where children have suffered from lack of physical nurturing and comfort as a baby.) Very often people complain to me about a boy who kicks repeatedly. If this boy is given the opportunity to kick where it is acceptable, say a pile of boxes, he will be better placed to make a good decision about where to kick next time he needs to do it. Kicking is no longer bad but the choice of where to do it gives the boys back some control. Allow Adapt Add (Hanen).

Allow the boy to kick but Adapt it to an acceptable place. Finally give him the opportunity for a hobby or Add a sport that includes kicking. You will both feel so much better and have much less conflict.

An example that helped me to understand a little of how this 'need to move' feels was when we had a big fall of snow last winter. There was simply no option . . . my boys were out of bed quicker than ever before and outside in the snow without question. It would have been cruel to try and stop them. They just had to do it. Another example was when I took five boys between six and eleven to London for the day. We went on a 'bendy bus' for the first time. There simply was no question of sitting down. We *all* had to stand on the articulated disc in the centre.

Wouldn't it be magical if schools could take the passion of these experiences and build on it in everyday teaching . . .? We can! We simply need to understand where these boys are coming from and have the passion to challenge, to share our understanding, to make the difference.

If we are able to carry this through we will be living my dream, four simple words 'Less stress . . . more passion'. Isn't this how you would like to live, learn, teach and work? I truly believe it is possible. What a different world we would live in.

Target sports

Whether or not as a legacy from hunting, boys are typically good at aiming at targets. Consider this, a teacher is standing at the front of the class. She has been talking for some time and 'Luke' is less than focused. A man walks past the window carrying a ladder. 'Luke' is drawn to movement, a legacy from his hunting forefathers? He wants to look at the man walking past the window. Because binocular vision in males and females is better when looking directly at an object, let's say around a 30-degree focus, Luke turns his head to have a clear view of his 'target', the man. The teacher notices his head movement, feels he is off task and most likely reprimands him in front of the class.

'Chloe' sitting next to Luke has seen the same man. She has more tolerance for the teacher's long introduction and can also use both hemispheres of her brain together to multi task. Her vision is more frequently used in a wider range, around 180 degrees, perhaps as a legacy of having to watch many children in a community hearth setting. She keeps facing the teacher and can also see the man. The difference is she keeps her head still and seems to be focused on the teacher. Chloe does not get reprimanded by the teacher nor humiliated in front of her peers.

Consider how these tendencies could affect an older boy or young man in a social setting.

In a social group a man sees an attractive woman enter his peripheral vision. He wants a sharper view and almost involuntarily turns his head to get a better look at her.

Consider the same situation; this time a woman sees an attractive man enter her peripheral vision. Her head stays still. She appears to remain focused, carries on two conversations and still gets a really good look at his shoes. (I haven't yet worked out why shoes are such a priority for women but I'm working on it!)

The different outcomes of these two scenarios could explain why many more young men are accused of being flirts and often worse, also why they are more prone to being physically challenged by men who may feel they are interested in their girlfriend. We need to warn teenage boys of these dangers and how to avoid them but also help adults better understand each other and to talk before they judge or act in trying to support stronger and longer-lasting relationships within which to raise good boys.

In order to hit moving targets, men would be skilled at judging speed and distance, especially of a deer or quarry ahead of them. This is something to remember when men and women differ in their tolerance of each other's driving style. (The other thing to remember is that men are also more likely to take risks!)

When searching for something, men look for characteristic features in their acute 'target range' of vision and see things less clearly outside that range (David Jones, optical advisor at Essilor). Women often find it frustrating that

Points for Action – Respect, Understanding and Relationships – Physical Activity

 Be sure to use sport as a positive forum for praise. Beware of the dangers of critical touchline dads and vociferous coaches and be there to support boys when they experience failure. Help them use the experience positively to build back the steps towards success.

Use Allow Adapt Add if a boy is repeatedly repeating a behaviour or action.

Help boys to develop strategies to understand the way they view their world and strategies to find things more easily.

Be tolerant of boys' head movement and help young adults to be aware of its dangers in social settings.

Look closely at boys who are bullied – do the adults around him communicate with him and treat him with respect, especially in front of others?

boys and men cannot find things whereas when women go to look they find it straight away. Women tend to scan a wider field of vision and often have a visual memory for where things are kept. Men look for a specific characteristic and if that is not clearly visible then they consider the item unlikely to be there. Pease et al. suggest that this is why men cannot find the butter in the fridge!

An interesting connection with the animal world is that predators tend to have their eyes on the front of their head for optimum binocular vision whereas prey have their eyes on the sides of their head for a wider field of vision (Jones). Do men historically act as predators or prey? Does this affect how they see the world?

Bigger and better

Respectful leadership

When hunting, men will work as a team towards a shared goal but there is always a leader. That leader is only effective if he is respected and in order to be respected a man has to earn his position and be seen to deserve it. As we have discovered in Chapter 9 boys are more likely to look to their dads for leadership from the age of six. This can cause challenges for female teachers and mums. Many of the women I have worked with have noticed that boys of this age are less likely to do what they are asked by a woman, especially if there is another boy around. (It is important that we talk to our boys about this and help them recognize this behaviour in order to find ways to overcome it.) Communication and discipline based on respect will make a big difference here in fact, it goes without saying that respectful communication is paramount in all relationships in families, in schools and in communities.

Bullying

Boys will challenge others in order to move themselves up in the perceived ranking of their peer group. They are wise and will only challenge those they perceive to be weaker than them, those they feel they have a chance of defeating. This does not have to be a physical challenge, it often shows itself in verbal and psychological challenge in other words . . . bullying. This *has* to be nipped in the bud and those on the receiving end supported (as well as those giving it out). If his behaviour is perpetuating the bullying, a boy needs help and support to learn more appropriate behaviours. If a boy does not feel truly listened to and actively supported his whole demeanour reflects this. This demeanour is the very thing that is picked up by those wishing to be seen as dominant and the cycle continues. How many of us as parents or teachers can stand proud and say we've never responded to a child's pleas with a sigh or with a 'not again Luke'?

> Boys will only challenge those they perceive to be weaker than them.

Failure

Boys need help to deal with failure and see it as part of learning. Simple card games are a perfect start for this as they encourage all kinds of valuable social skills as well as how to handle losing with grace. Ortberg empowered me with strategies to face up to failure, supporting my students if they were struggling.

Sometimes when a boy is perceived to fail he has simply taken a wrong route. Failure is an opportunity to reflect and find a positive way forward. It is important that we only expose boys to the risk of failure if we feel they have the self-esteem and confidence to pick themselves up when they are unsuccessful. If he really wants to achieve the goal and is struggling, he may need encouragement to take a different route or reassess where he wants to end up. We can help boys to see their way out of failure by using the acronym FIX.

FIX

F is for Facts	Clearly state the facts avoiding the word 'you'. This avoids the boy feeling blamed.
I is for I	I feel . . . Ask the boy how these facts make him feel and tell him how you feel using the words 'I feel'.
X is about fixing the problem	See the X as the linked arms of two people, side by side. It symbolizes how you and the boy will work together to find a positive solution to the problem.

Taking risks

In hunting, it is vital to take risks. If you never fire an arrow you will never kill your prey. Boys need to take risks to learn what their growing bodies are capable of, especially if they have recently had a surge of testosterone.

Boys are more likely to have injuries than girls; it could be due to this fact that boys have less nerve endings in their skin (Pease et al.).

Men are likely to get scratched or cut on hunting trips. They also seem to dismiss these injuries more easily than girls. (Dads need to be sensitive that when their daughter says it really hurts . . . it does!)

Can you imagine a man coming back from a hunting trip to tell his family that he did not kill the bison as there was a patch of brambles in the way! In risk taking some men would be happier to die trying rather than come home unsuccessful.

Could this lesser number of nerve endings be a possible reason why many young boys cannot feel if they have food around their mouth at meal times, or don't feel uncomfortable if their shirt is untucked? This lower level of sensitivity in comparison with girls is often questioned in relation to so-called 'man–flu'. Why is it if a woman gets a cold she plods on, and 'gets over it'? Men are more likely to take to their beds. Why the difference?

Consider this from the legacy of hunting . . . How would it be if the whole team of hunters have to stop because Luke has 'a bit of a headache' and needs to sit down? How would that go down in the 'bigger and better man culture'? I suggest that men have to make a clear decision, they are either ill or they are not. Men often get frustrated with women who 'soldier on' expecting sympathy. Men rarely do this and find it difficult to understand. Women in the communal hearth still had to look after the children, ill or not and in many situations the same rings true today. A man's perspective is more likely to be, if you are ill you go to bed, if you are up and about you are better. How far will this little snippet of knowledge help in relationships if both parties understand where the other is coming from?

> As far as a man is concerned if you are ill you go to bed, if you are up and about you are better.

We need to offer more opportunities for boys to take risks under our 'umbrella of safety'. They may get hurt but more likely, in trying out what their minds and bodies can achieve they will not have to try this out by running across railway lines to prove their strength to their gang later in life. I believe that every school should have a 'Risk and Responsibility' or 'Seize Opportunities Safely' policy agreed with parents, teachers and children. It should involve members of the community and encourage them to engage with our children safely both in and outside of school. It would be part of PACCT (Parents, Adults, Children, Communities and Teachers).

Parks and open spaces need to be seen to be safer places, perhaps with active wardens or play leaders who will allow boys and girls alike to try new things and take risks in an appropriate environment. Parents need to pay less attention to the media and, knowing their community is reasonably safe and supporting, allow boys more freedom to play out, take risks and also take the responsibility that goes hand in hand with these risks.

Embracing communities

I suggest that everyone should implement a PACCT in their community.

Parents, adults, children, communities and teachers all committing to work together through PACCT; schools need to be open and welcoming to all members of the community. We know this needs to be carefully handled with police checks etc., but driven positively it *can* happen. Here are just some

---

PACCT

- All ages of community members *actively* welcomed into the school to help in specific and non-specific ways to meet many of their needs as well as those of the children and each other. (Perhaps they could register their interests on a database of skills and talents.)
- Events are to be organized for all PACCT members.
- Community police, youth leaders, religious groups, toddler groups, childminders etc. All keen to be involved and willing to share the extended school's philosophy for the future should be welcomed.
- All PACCT members to be police checked, registered on the school's database and regularly updated with e-mail or hand-delivered newsletter.
- Willing PACCT members to display a sticker with a registration number in a clearly visible window in their home. Register of these addresses to be available on PACCT website for all PACCT members.
- PACCT members actively encouraged to greet each other. (This seems such a simple thing to write and almost ludicrous, however, it is amazing how many parents with children at the same school pass each other each morning and do not even make eye contact let alone smile. The difference this greeting would make is far greater than it seems initially.)
- PACCT members to be invited to share a community meal at the school on a regular basis (at least once a month) to encourage them to feel welcome and involved.
- PACCT members to get local discounts with their membership card and all members to benefit from group purchase discounts (theatre tickets, holiday discounts . . . the list is endless).
- Ex-pupils welcomed as members of PACCT to support activities and share their successes.
- PACCT policy to include sharing the school's positive approach to a better understanding and brighter future for boys.
- PACCT in the PARK could use creative solutions based on this network to make parks safer and more vibrant places.

Benefits of PACCT

- Children in the community will know that homes displaying registered stickers will be willing to offer help if a child is in crisis. (Guidelines will need to be agreed about children's safety for entering other people's homes.)
- Children and parents feel safer in their local community.
- Community members will feel welcomed in their schools and encouraged to offer help.
- Trusted men will feel safe and supported in order to volunteer and make such a difference to the future of boys and those who care for them.
- Boys (and girls) will know older children in the community and have tangible 'Local Heroes' as positive role models.
- Community members will get to know other local PACCT members and build networks to support their needs.
- Lone, isolated and new parents will feel welcomed and supported.
- All members of our communities will feel more at ease offering to help and asking for help, something so many boys and men find difficult.
- Parents (whether working or at home) and children will know other families who live close to them and can build networks of support and friendship.

Monitoring of PACCT

- Window stickers to be clearly visible with registration number and PACCT telephone number/ community police link clearly displayed.
- PACCT members registered with local police and the school (ways to check this out will need to be agreed).
- PACCT members need to be involved in school in order for their faces to be familiar and the members known to the school community.
- Local postal workers, milk providers or community wardens to be involved in the scheme through monitoring the stickers in their area. Their involvement in PACCT and the school to be encouraged through a WELCOME policy inviting them to 'bacon butties and hot chocolate' at the school at least once a month.

potential ways forward, but remember your school and local community is full of creativity to find solutions to match your individual situation!

I believe passionately in PACCT and, while I have made several suggestions, *you* will be the ones to know how best to move forward for your school. My best advice for you would be to overcome any doubts about the challenges it faces and to think big. I believe that PACCT, once initiated, brings with it its own momentum and solutions, and the benefits alone could fill a book.

This section is about taking risks. I believe that all schools need to take the risk of launching into PACCT. There will be some hurdles and some stumbles but, if driven with a passion for the future the benefits will show us all that the risk was worthwhile.

The big outdoors

Boys have so many skills that are happiest when outdoors. Boys and dads love camping, adventurous activities, so many things concerned with fresh air and nature. Many schools with policies to include outdoor education really benefit from this, whether it is a rough area of land turned over to building dens and simply investigating, growing their own vegetables, nurturing school animals such as chickens or even having a school dog. I was delighted to be asked to help design an outdoor music garden with Stoughton Nursery School. We used big equipment that we found around the school and the children helped to change the way it works on a daily basis. It is magnetic to these young children, especially the boys who have outlets to make noise, experiment with sounds and use their gross motor skills to full effect.

There are several things with close links to the 'big outdoors' that have magnetic attractions for boys . . . trees, water and fire. I find it strange that the things boys so gravitate to are very powerful when used with skill and care but can be extremely dangerous if approached without appropriate guidance or a watchful eye.

Fires

Fires are all powerful. I do not know a male of any age who can walk past a bonfire without prodding it or seeing if he can get a stick to burn. It could also explain the fact that, if there is a barbeque, a man will most likely be in charge of it. Fire along with sticks and stones are powerful tools for boys. They gravitate towards them but need to learn how to use them safely. They need to be able to observe a skilled craftsman honing his blade in order to be able to use these tools safely for himself. We no longer use flints and stone axes but boys still need to learn how to use the tools of today from a trusted mentor. Where does this fit into our busy lives at home or at school?

Fires are at the centre of gatherings; men tell stories of the hunt or how big was the one that got away. If men need to solve problems they also frequently go 'within their own head' and 'fire gaze'. They are unlikely to be able to hear anything else. Women talk to solve problems and many believe men should do the same! How many women interrupt men when they are silent, asking them to share their thoughts? How many teachers tell off the boy who is figuratively fire gazing?

Things that move

In the hunt, how would the men get a large bison home? They would have to design and build some sort of framework to transport it back to the clan . . . only a short step from designing the go-karts in Chapter 2. Men's strengths in things spatial and visual, along with the scientific angle makes projects with transport a real winner when involving dads.

A little aside . . . (If we have any doubt that testosterone and its effects have a bearing on visual and spatial ability consider the following anecdote:

Maureen, a lady of mature years was fascinated by the perceived differences in many skills between males and females. She was at a stage in life where the estrogen levels had dropped making her underlying testosterone levels more apparent. She was amazed when she understood the reasoning behind some-thing she had recently observed in herself.

'Since the menopause I have been able to read maps and parallel park. I was never able to do these things before!'

Women of a certain age . . . there is hope for the future!)

> 'Since the menopause I have been able to read maps and parallel park!'

Transport seems to ring all the bells for boys, it is mostly outdoors; vehicles can be tested, competed, fine tuned and they meet the desire of boys to dis-cover how things work and how fast they can go. There is also the thrill of the risk taking when you test it out for the first time – will the boy or the dad have to test out the go-kart first?. . . I wonder!

'Projects with a purpose'

One of the best ways we can motivate trusted men to work alongside growing boys in schools is to be sure they have 'projects with a purpose'. (This also works when engaging boys to help around the house.) Males communicate best when there is a shared task and they can talk about how their projects are progressing. As they spend more time together their trust and respect will grow. They will learn from each other and enjoy each other's company. If this is in place as part of an everyday situation then when the boy needs someone to turn to, there will be a trusted person to ask for first-hand male help. If it is really difficult to get good trusted men involved do keep trying. We would not think of teaching a child French at school and never allowing them the opportunity to visit the country and spend time with the locals.

> It is so much better for a boy to learn the skills of being a man from someone who has 'smelled the air' at first hand.

Success breeds success

The more we encourage boys to work on projects with a purpose the more there will be success. We are very quick in Western society to reprimand, blame and punish. We need to turn around that culture and celebrate our successes. (Remember Anger Blame Condemn turns into Stop Think, Understand and Value from Chapter 5.) Schools need to focus on the positives and encourage boys to be proud of their achievements.

We need to be very careful here with children who have special needs, the majority of whom are boys. I have always been uneasy with the 'special needs' description as I believe every person has special needs. I certainly have no desire to belittle the fact that some children have considerably more challenges than others but would it not be better to label the groups and places we support them in as 'focus' units?

We know boys are very vulnerable to criticism and it is important for them to be able to stand proud in front of their peers. If we label a child as 'special needs' it is very easy to see the label alone, as if a blanket were covering the individual that lies beneath it. If we describe the child as needing a special focus or focused support then this will help us work with *individuals* who have a specific learning style or groups with a shared need for a social skills focus. These focuses can be achieved through motivating the boy to take on challenges that break him through his previous glass ceiling. These boys could then be seen as children rather than viewed by the labels of dyslexic, ADHD, disruptive or lower ability. The focus units could also be used for boys running a mini enterprise or a group of children needing focus support to design and produce their own school journal (gifted and talented). I suggest for the very best use of these units and departments that they have an open-door policy. They need to work very closely with the family support leader to understand and agree the specific focus and empower the parent to work hand in hand with the school and its support services.

The more 'projects with a purpose' we put in place (or even better allow boys to initiate) the more opportunities there will be for raised self-esteem, increased confidence and to celebrate success.

Boys need to see other boys succeeding in order to have real-life heroes. Success is a frame of mind. If you believe you can succeed you are much more likely to do so. If you have experienced success you will want more of it and seek opportunities to succeed. The experiences of those successes will also help you to be strong on the occasions that success is slow to come.

If success is difficult to achieve it may be you are pursuing the wrong project. If you simply *have* to do it, then think positive and get 'into it'.

> If you can't get out of it get into it!

I heard a stunt actor describing how she avoided getting hurt. She said that you don't give up when you are half way over the hedge. If you have experienced success then you are more likely to 'give it your all' as you know how worthwhile it is to see a project through to completion.

To celebrate success, every school, every class, every PACCT, every family and every boy should have a 'Brag book'. We all need to share what is going well and encourage our local press to do the same. Success needs to become part of our culture.

Points of Action – Respect, Understanding and Relationships – The Big Outdoors

Be understanding of boys and men who are 'fire-gazing' even if there is no fire . . . they may well be solving problems.

Transport appeals to most males in some way. Use this creatively for activities that get men and boys working together, especially in the big outdoors.

Remember 'projects with a purpose', especially valuable to engage demotivated boys in school, and at home and to encourage 'men as mentors'.

Success is a frame of mind. Boys need to see other boys succeeding to have real-life 'Local Heroes'.

Be bold, encourage your boys to keep and share 'Brag books' and celebrate success in the local press . . . then they will know what they are proud of. Success needs to become part of our culture.

Being focused

'Saying no'

How often do adults say 'no' to boys? In homes parents often say no if they want to play out . . . it's not safe. In communities adults say 'no' if boys want to kick a ball in the street . . . they might upset the neighbours. In school teachers say 'no' to boys who want to install a climbing wall . . . it is too expensive, people might be silly, we have to do a risk assessment, who would build it?

Over recent years adults have got into the habit of saying 'no' especially in schools, when people are too busy, when parents are bringing up boys alone, when adults are worried about the risks.

> Over recent years we have got into the habit of saying 'no' to boys.

I believe, at schools and at home, boys have stopped asking. I believe they have lost their impulsiveness because of the challenges of twenty-first-century lives. Is it any wonder that they have lost their motivation, their direction and their passion? Is it any wonder they stop asking and gravitate to the things that keep them quiet and out of trouble, to the safety of screens?

They get so much from screens. The games take them to a world where they can experience adventure, where they have some control. The games most boys like involve some kind of fighting, racing, heroes, things they are not allowed to do in the real world but hark back to the legacy of the hunter; they allow boys to be all consumed and single-minded.

> 'The way you think is the way you behave' (Ortberg).

How would it be if the word 'no' was removed from our vocabularies and our way of thinking and, within reason, replaced with 'maybe', 'after half term' or even 'yes'? What if the adults followed this through and made things happen? I feel excited just thinking about it. If we change the way we think and take notice of the positive possibilities it is amazing how easy it becomes to make things happen.

In hunting, boys had to be impulsive. They did not harp back to the time that their colleague got injured. They simply got on with it and . . . surprise surprise, most of the time it was successful.

> If a herd of antelope came along the men did not sit down and do a risk assessment!

I am in no way suggesting that we take unnecessary risks with the lives of young boys but is saying 'yes' occasionally and finding ways to make it happen so radical?

Begin with the boys

How does this help teachers to follow the curriculum in school? They need to be flexible. They need to start with the children and be sure the curriculum meets their needs. They need to look at the areas that can be learned through practical, vibrant approaches and prescribe appropriate solutions where a focus is needed. They need to involve the children, asking them what *they* want to learn about a project. They need to be enthusiastic and creative about the things that have simply got to be learned and break these up with fun activities and things that the boys, the girls and the teachers themselves enjoy.

Schools need to know their boys so much better and, male or female, *all staff* need to understand the ways they may think, learn and behave. In order to achieve this I would strongly recommend classes of no more than 24. In the interim a teaching assistant in *every* class, working to their strengths to support the teacher and the children should be compulsory.

The prescriptive curriculum

The prescriptive curriculum and emphasis on testing have shackled teachers for too long. It can, unless presented creatively, quash children's 'hunger for learning'. As an analogy, if we simply have to get children to eat peas there are many more creative ways of achieving this than simply putting peas in front of them every single day and expecting them to chew. This approach is having the effect of children simply not wanting to 'eat'.

> The prescriptive curriculum and emphasis on testing have shackled teachers for too long.

Through better understanding boys' teachers will feel empowered to release the shackles. They will have the drive and momentum to use their creativity and passion for teaching, for children, for boys, for the future.

Just say it

When hunting which of the following would a man be most likely to say . . . ?

'Excuse me Luke, I think there's a group of gazelles about to cross over the hill, you know the one where we caught the hog least season. Would you mind gathering up your spears and coming along with me to see if we can bag one for lunch?'

Or

'Luke. Gazelle on hill. Go.'

We spoke about women being wordy and men being succinct in Chapter 7, but when you link this to the hunting legacy it does seem to make sense. When boys are given instructions they need to be succinct and to the point. Parents and educators need to give instructions one at once when boys are little tired or stressed making sure of good eye contact to ensure they can hear. (There may well be a stage at the age of fourteen when the brain connections are reconfiguring to drive the adult body and simple respectful instructions help immensely.) Women need to rely less heavily on non-verbal cues as these are difficult for boys to read and cause frustration and misunderstanding. The number of instructions can be built up gradually as boys develop strategies to help them remember.

Are schools too wordy?

Are schools too wordy?

Consider these questions in the light of what you now know about the way many males function:

- Do schools and teachers communicate with boys in ways that are easy for them to access?
- Do teachers allow boys to record their work in ways that match their way of thinking?
- Are potential male teachers overwhelmed by wordy staff meetings, documentation and demands for planning that could easily be a thesis?
- Are there ways to help teachers, of whatever sex, record things in a way that suits their own style of thinking?
- Are there ways that teachers could work without necessarily having to multi task?
- How could more good male teachers be encouraged into the profession and into schools generally?

When you have decided what your school needs to do you will be well placed to empower more trusted men to make things better for boys.

Then all you need is PUMA:

- Passion
- Understanding
- Motivation
- Action

Advocates for boys

I recommend that every school with boys from six or seven have an advocate for boys and their needs. (No doubt there would be a similar advocate for girls and their needs.) This advocate would most likely hold another role in the school but it would be his job to ensure that the school, through its curriculum and teaching styles as well as through its PACCT provision was offering the very best provision for boys. He would have a depth of understanding about what boys need and keep up to date with good practice and research in the field. He would access and input a website to network with other advocates to share and spread the exciting initiatives proving successful for the future of boys across the world. He would be a point of reference for teachers, parents and all members of PACCT who work with boys or who need support for a challenge they are facing with their boys. He would be actively engaged with many of the activities designed to match the needs of boys and, of course, he would be a fabulous role model!

Points for Action – Man as Hunter – The Big Outdoors

Give clear simple instructions to boys at the time they need them. Be sure to gain respectful eye contact to ensure they can hear you.

Promote creativity, passion and purpose in all teaching, especially for boys.

Find creative ways to employ more good male teachers while respecting and valuing the women teachers who really understand and care about boys.

Recruit or appoint a dynamic 'Advocate for Boys' in every school with boys over seven.

Find opportunities to say 'yes' to boys at home, at school and in communities. Use PUMA (Passion Understanding Motivation Action) to make it happen!

Man as mentor

Boys need men!

There is currently a void in the lives of many boys. Although there is a great deal of good, however supportive, understanding, caring or dynamic women are (and I count myself in this) there are certain things that boys need from men at first hand.

I observed a wonderful moment at my breakfast table last week. My eldest son has recently moved school and now wears a tie. His dad was respectfully showing him how to go about getting your tie to look cool and avoid having a huge long tail that could dip in your porridge. My attention was not on the tie 'master class' but on my second son. He had stopped eating and was absolutely transfixed on this lesson of 'how to be a guy and get it right'. You could almost read the admiration across his forehead and the thoughts ' I'm going to be a man soon so I'd better tune in'.

I love my boys to bits and did wear a tie as part of my school uniform, but, there is no way, as a woman, I would ever be able to show my son a simple tie knot and make it involve all the subplot about 'how to be a cool man' and 'I'm so proud of the way you are growing up' that went on in that special two minutes with my husband.

I am not suggesting that 'crunchy bix' put a handy-sized father figure in every box of cereal but I am strongly suggesting that parents and teachers find creative ways to involve men constructively in the lives of every single boy they care for.

Please feel free to come up with wild and wondrous plans that match the unique needs of your boys, your families, your schools (do share your successes through the website www.mibfb.com) but in the meantime I offer framework that holds true promise for sustained and sustainable mentoring. I call it SAGE.

SAGE

Mission

To provide a forum for boys of different ages to work together within a consistent supporting and supported group led and mentored by an adult of the same gender working towards specific purposes and nurturing passions.

The theory is simple:

- SAGE stands for SAme GEnder. It also describes a wise person.
- Two boys from each year group are linked together in family-type SAGE groups.
- Each SAGE group has an assigned mentor of the same gender.
- The SAGE group sits at a round table, eats and talks together once a fortnight (eight boys).
- Once a month their SAGE mentor comes to join them for lunch.

A little more detail

All members of the SAGE group are expected and encouraged to reflect on the following three areas:

Skills   What am I good at? What skills do I have? What skills do my family have?

Scope   What am I able to get better at right now?

Service   How can I help/support/mentor others with my skills?

All boys to keep their own scrapbook or 'Brag Book' to hold tangibly what they are good at, what they are passionate about and where their scope lies for the future – they could include a hopes and wishes list.

It is the responsibility of every SAGE member to 'look out' for their team in the playground and report any concerns to their SAGE leader or boys advocate.

SAGE members to attend assemblies to celebrate their team members' successes. (Perhaps SAGE groups could be the framework for house groups and special assemblies.)

Sage members to be in the same classes and to work frequently with their parallel female pairing. Male and female groups may decide to work on some projects or 'celebrations' together.

Every child in the school should be embraced as part of a SAGE group.

Format and purpose of SAGE meeting

To meet regularly as part of a non-judgemental, supportive team
All relationships within the SAGE scheme to be based on respect
Each meeting to have its time protected. It should be seen as a priority

Each monthly meeting to follow this framework:

1. Successes and Smiles (including reflection from previous meeting)
2. Sadnesses and Struggles (including reflection from previous meeting)
3. Solutions (looking at creative realistic ways to solve problems within the group and in the community)
4. Scope (looking forward to what the group and individuals would like to achieve, both for themselves and for others. Value and draw on the resources and skills each boy has available within his family)
5. 'Celebrations'. Plan something fun for the group or the community. (Some boys never experience treats and they don't have to cost anything.)

One scrapbook/ brag book to be kept centrally for each SAGE group
Mentor to steer the meeting and encourage older four boys to take a responsible lead

Resource implications

Length of lunchtimes
Circular adult – height tables and adjustable height chairs
Scrap books
Mobile phones and computer access for mentors
Training, support and security checks

Issues and benefits for transition

Summer Term

SAGE group to make a welcome pack for their new younger members – it should be very personal to their group.

SAGE groups to visit infant schools once a year to share their projects, passions and successes (Local Heroes for younger boys).

Year five SAGE group members go to the infant school to visit their new members in class and to have lunch with them.

The day the eldest two members visit secondary school the next two members are invited to join the SAGE group for lunch from their infant school. These two boys play a lead role in showing the new boys around the school.

Autumn Term

SAGE mentor meets and eats with his previous SAGE members once a week at their new secondary school possibly at breakfast? This reduces after half term as appropriate to the relationship but contact is maintained every half term, face to face or by phone. (The SAGE mentor is such a vital support in this first term.)

SAGE members are welcomed back at their junior school to help, for support or as 'Local Heroes'.

Some small but important detail

Boys must remain at the table for at least half an hour (implications on the school schedule to be considered).

Table manners are modelled and encouraged.

Tables are prepared to look welcoming by second eldest SAGE members.

Mentor needs to see this link as a long-term commitment, two years would be a suggested minimum.

Mentors should be matched to their group by the boys' advocate and be responsible to him.

Mentors should be respected volunteers but should not be expected to contribute financially to any meals or celebrations.

Mentor has no expectation to help in class or outside his SAGE group activities but would be welcomed should he wish to do so.

Mentor and group are encouraged to involve other trusted adults as agreed by all members of the group.

SAGE groups are rather like families – no member should ever be left out or excluded. Solving problems together would be part of the group's brief.

Hiccups – a few no doubt but worth overcoming.

Benefits – too vast to list . . . try a brainstorm if you have any doubts!

Why do we need men as mentors?

- 'In 2006 in Britain, more than 200 pupils under 11 were sent home each day for bad behaviour at school, sixty boys aged four were expelled and one-tenth of all teenage boys have been suspended at some time for bad behaviour' (Julie Greenhough, *Times Ed*, 18 May 2007).
  These boys need rudders for their boats.
  Men as mentors through SAGE can give them direction, stability and purpose.
- 'If there are gangs of boys on your streets then the older men in the community are not doing their job' (*Manhood*, Biddulph).
  Men as mentors through SAGE can offer trusted adult males safe purposeful ways to 'do their job' and make a real difference to the future of boys.
- Transition is one of the most vulnerable times in a boy's education. Too many stumble at this fence.
  Men as mentors through SAGE can change that giving stability across transitions.
- Many boys have no trusted males in their lives.
  Men as mentors through SAGE can change that offering boys and their families trusted male mentors in safe, supportive situations.
- Boys glued to screens often struggle with social skills and have little passion in life.
  Men as mentors through SAGE can change that with social skills being a key part of SAGE groups.

- Schools are being tasked with involving communities and supporting families.
  SAGE addresses both of these and makes life better for boys and all involved with them.
- Businesses are being encouraged to implement 'social responsibility policies'. Business people are actively seeking opportunities to 'make a difference'.
  SAGE can give them those opportunities and they can make a difference to our boys and their future.

It's got to be worth a try!

The way to a man's heart – food as the key to the future

> Food is such a powerful resource we need to seize it as the key to making our schools welcoming places where families and communities can refuel, refresh and regenerate.

Providing fuel

A man's body is a powerful thing. There are analogies with driving fast cars (Chapter 8) but a car is no good if it is short on fuel. A man simply has to eat. Men and boys frequently get hunger pains and find it almost impossible to focus on anything other than where their next meal is coming from. There is little point expecting men or boys to function effectively unless they are well fuelled. Schools are well placed to provide fuel for boys, for men and for the families who are so crucial to their well-being and success.

When I began teaching I was given a valuable piece of advice . . . the caretaker is the most important person in the school. Without the caretaker little else in a school can be effective. I suggest now that another member of staff is key to the future of PACCT schools . . . the chef. This person will need to embrace the PACCT culture (Chapter 11) and will have the opportunity to really make their schools the heart of the community. They will need to be creative, open, willing, flexible and caring.

At The Mount School the success of their extended services centres around food, their chef and his flexibility. There is never a case of turning a child (or a parent) away. The chef knows the families that are in need and is quick to welcome hungry children with 'your mum's paid . . . choose whatever you like'.

> The school chef will have the opportunity to really make their schools the heart of the community.

The school uses creative fundraising and charitable support to make this possible in an area of social need.

The best schools have always looked out for children but now they need to be all embracing. Sunderland stresses the importance of nurture for parents; surely for stressed and exhausted parents, whatever the reasons behind their stresses, food is a huge part of being nurtured, especially if they have no family or support networks nearby. Shopping, cooking and eating all take up valuable time. If schools can offer fabulous simple food and opportunities for parents and children to share these, they are not only making it better for boys but for all the people who care for them.

Think of the places where you feel most welcome, most at ease . . . are these places where you are offered a warm drink, a snack, invited to share a meal and a smile?

Wouldn't it be wonderful if, we as members of PACCT schools, extend them to embrace communities, that everyone feels welcomed, at ease, happy to be part of our school, supportive of our families?

The SAGE mentor groups suggested in Chapter 11 are centred around food. So many exciting and powerful opportunities are within our reach with food as the key. You could see it as putting the dining table back at the centre of our lives.

> . . . putting the dining table back at the centre of our lives.

Companions

This scheme to support boys and communities could begin in infant schools or even nurseries. Each class of children could have a COMPANION, the meaning of the word deriving directly from 'sharing bread with'. This could be an older person from the community who would move with the children as they travel through their school career. Each year as they move to a new teacher they benefit from the consistency of a caring 'companion' who knows the children well and what is successful for them. They would be someone the children could talk to and each week that the 'companion' is in school they are welcomed to share time with the teacher, perhaps having breakfast or coffee before school. Breaktime or after the time spent with the class could be sharing tasks such as gardening or costume making with other companions, building friendships and networks. Lunchtime would most certainly be, eating at a table and getting to really know the children. There are many benefits to this scheme but I suggest one of the greatest ones for boys is that of learning mutual respect through relationships with caring people of all generations.

'The Respect Agenda' emphasizes the need for respect across generations and so many older people would love to get involved with young children but struggle to find safe, appropriate ways in. Older people all have different strengths and, if these are nurtured the children, the teachers, the children and the future relationships between boys and members of the community would benefit enormously. I recommend that each class should have at least two companions, ideally one of each sex and a balance to match the cultural backgrounds of the children. They should follow the children across transitions and certainly on to the beginning of secondary education. If one is unable to continue for any reason there must be another companion put in place for those children. The relationships are all important. The schools will build relationships with the companions and no doubt be there for them in times of difficulty but what benefits will this new older dimension bring to our rich school communities of the future!

A huge challenge for boys today is stress and lack of family time. Relieve stress for families and it will certainly make it better for boys.

Sharing meals

Sharing meals and activities is the way forward. It doesn't really matter which meal we are encouraging our PACCT members to share. If we are going to be offering care from 8 a.m. to 6 p.m. we may as well take these opportunities to build relationships between the school and families, between boys and girls, between parents and neighbours. Isn't this a better option than simply offering 8 to 6 'factory farmed childcare' distancing boys still further from their stressed and exhausted parents?

Patrick Leeson Head of Children's Services in the Royal Borough of Kingston upon Thames asks 'How can you support the child unless you support the family?'

Surely this 'open house' approach will go a long way to meeting this.

Breakfast is a meal that is often rushed or missed out by working parents. How would it be if we actually opened playgrounds for these parents to park while they eat a bacon butty (see appendix) and fresh fruit alongside their son. There could be salads and sandwiches for them to buy for lunch and even newspapers or book swaps available for the train journey. As long as the cars are gone before the playground is needed I'm sure many schools could make this successful and working parents would really appreciate this opportunity.

Parents walking their children to school could also join in at the breakfast club. They may join their child in a calm activity a 'personal pursuit' they could pick up and put down easily such as Lego models, puzzles, crosswords, origami etc. Parents may welcome the opportunity to talk to a health visitor, housing support officer, financial adviser, parent support worker . . . the list goes on. They may choose to stay and get involved in helping in classes or at a stay and play session. Busy parents may find it useful to drop off their ironing, meet their childminder, buy birthday cards, find a babysitter on the PACCT notice-board . . . .

The opportunities for PACCT schools to support parents of all kinds are endless.

Listening to parents

It is important that your PACCT school takes initiatives but even more important is to listen to parents and ask what *they* really need. Every individual must be valued for what *they* can offer. Whether it is administrative services and parcel collection for working parents, teatime swaps for lone parents or access to the jobseekers website; whatever services you are able to offer will improve relationships, health and make parents' lives happier and less stressful. If through these simple things we can make family life so much better it will benefit everyone, especially boys.

Listen to parents and ask what *they* really need.

The extended school day

There are opportunities all through the school day to use great simple food and a welcoming team to make such a difference. We have mentioned welcoming postal and delivery workers and community members of all ages. We could welcome expectant parents, young parents, grandparents and those who would simply love to be part of the life of the school.

Lunchtime offers opportunities for parents, companions, mentors and teachers to eat with children, but also, if viewed creatively, we can offer opportunities for flexibility to help with some of the struggles parents and teachers have to fit everything in. If we were able to allow ninety minutes or even two hours for lunchtime then, with advance agreement, a parent could take a child to the dentist, for a swim together or even out for lunch. Teachers could work some lunch times and have the benefit of flexibility to nurture themselves or their own families in the ones they choose to take off. (I realize this seems rather radical and would take careful management but unless we think outside the box we may be constrained by convention and tradition.) The other positive of a longer lunchtime would be a focus on the *occasion* of eating, social skills, perhaps sharing a table with a teacher and having some time to get to know each other as human beings. I detest mealtimes where children are growled at and not even allowed to sit next to a friend for fear they might talk and slow down the conveyor belt of children. Many are rushed out before they have had a chance to chew let alone enjoy their mealtime!

> Teachers could have the benefit of flexibility to nurture themselves or their own families.

At lunch break children would have a good length of time to take part in a leisure activity, music, sport, cycle maintenance . . . as well as time to play, then time to wind down with a calm activity, listening to music or perhaps relaxation exercises alongside their teacher before embarking on their afternoon calm and nourished and well placed for more effective, dynamic learning.

After school there would be activities that children and adults can do separately or together. There would be opportunities for parents and children to eat together . . . something simple but nourishing that would not waste if it did not all get used . . . a slow cooked casserole, a pasta bake, a hearty soup, all reasonably priced and using cheaper seasonal – produce food that does not need a qualified chef to serve and store. Alongside this a selection of ready meals, familiar to the children, that parents can buy from the freezer or cooler for a quick yet healthy meal back home.

There are just so many opportunities and, while they make things better for all children, boys will benefit so much from having less stress, more time, better relationships and good food as part of their daily lives.

Teachers and food

There are opportunities in the day for teachers to use food towards building better relationships and getting to know their pupils as individuals. Playground duty is an opportunity to have a 'break buddy', a child chosen each time the teacher is on duty to walk and talk with them and share a treat of a chocolate biscuit! Teachers can follow a rota of children to be their buddy or a child may be obviously in need of a little extra time and attention rather than being punished.

At lunchtime, rather than missing out on playtime so much needed by boys, a child could sit and eat with the advocate or their teacher, then join a caring adult in the playground. After only a minute or two of dealing with why they behaved as they did and how this could be overcome, this method not only avoids stress and humiliation but soon becomes a pleasant time where both teacher and pupil learn valuable things about each other. Children who often go unnoticed can also benefit from this one to one time together.

> We all need to know that we are seen as individuals and not simply judged by our behaviour.

Benefits for boys

Many of these suggestions help everyone in schools. My final suggestions are *specifically* designed to help boys. Boys benefit immensely if they have a father or respected male giving them time, showing interest in them as a person and in their school work.

Homework SAGE

There is a strong link between good achievement and behaviour in school and the interest a father takes in his son's homework. We have looked at the need for purpose in a task so a combination of these things, along with food, can help us promote positive attitudes to work and self-belief as well as nurturing good relationships between boys and respected men.

Once a fortnight an enjoyable homework task with a specific purposeful focus could be set for a boy to do with his father or a father figure. That evening the pair should spend time eating together, either at school or at home, then go on to work on the specific SAGE Homework Task. The school could encourage trusted volunteers from the local community to get involved where there is no father figure, perhaps older members or local university or college students (these are often grateful for a good meal!). It is really important that the boy's mum or carer is involved in this liaison as the mentor has to have her trust and respect and vice versa. Hopefully, apart from all the other benefits of a mentor, these relationships may gradually build, offering abundant benefits to all involved. (With all these SAGE and mentor activities it is crucial that they are sustained across transition stages when boys will benefit hugely from the consistency at the time of change.)

Reading SAGE

This is similar to the homework SAGE but this mentor would cut in around the crucial age of six to seven. If a boy was showing little aptitude or interest in reading then a mentor of the same sex, perhaps from the local sixth form or through 'Help the Aged' or similar organization, would be encouraged to come and work with him at least twice a week to help him gain a love for reading and support him with the strategies put in place by the school. He may help him to focus on a passion he has and use this as a tool to generate a 'reason to read'. It is once again crucial that this partnership smoothes the transition from infant to junior school. A similar scheme has proved most effective at The Mount from age nine through to secondary school focusing on the boys most at risk of stumbling at the tricky hurdle of transition. The key to this relationship, once again is mentor and boy spending time eating together.

> Many boys need to discover a 'reason to read'.

Dads and lads

Activities, often adventurous, for dads and lads together are a tried and tested formula resulting in much success. It has been successfully run by parenting forums including a fabulous one in Surrey which runs activities for dads and lads on Saturdays. From my perspective it benefits from two adaptations. First it needs to be based around our PACCT schools supporting families in the local area. It must include food and meet the needs of the dads and lads but also address the obvious issue that families are not simply made up of dads and lads. Daughters should also be welcome if they wish and similar parallel activities need to be made available for mums and daughters with sons if they wish. The activities should be focused to meet the needs of the core group but also addressing that we now live in a world where both sexes need to be multi-skilled. Girls should be welcome to join in with building engines just as boys should be welcome to join in with more typically female activities.

What are the benefits of these group sessions?

- 'They see me solving problems with other adult males – how I overcome challenges and relate to others' (Chris, Dads and Lads, Dorking, Surrey).
- They offer opportunities for dads who only have contact with their boys at weekends.
- They give parents a focused useful activity that costs little or nothing.
- They help fathers and boys to develop a shared passion and purpose.
- They help them to relate and communicate together with less stress and greater respect.
- They empower boys and parents with skills they may find difficult to access.
- They afford opportunities for *boys to learn how to be men among other men*. . . .

Food is the key to the future . . . embrace it and enjoy!

Appendix – good food makes good guys

Thanks to Jamie Oliver and his mission for healthy eating we all know the benefit of wholemeal bread and good fresh veggies. Although I believe he has made a big difference to the eating habits of our children, when time is short, it is food and mealtimes that suffer first. If boys don't get the food they need they will find it for themselves and that is most likely to be through fast food and junk food.

Why is this such a big deal for boys? First boys are more susceptible to the side effects caused by so many 'E' numbers found in processed and snack food (many of which are banned in several countries). The medical journal *The Lancet* has researched some of the food additives that have been causing boys, especially those on the autistic spectrum, problems for many years. A cocktail of these commonly found additives can make boys behave as if they are about to explode. Fizzy drinks often make boys high but at last the effects of drinking squash are being acknowledged.

Water is crucial to our brains and bodies and most schools now are allowing children to have water in class. We should take this further and be sure to actually encourage water drinking and, parents or teachers, remember to drink it ourselves!

Most people know about the dangers of low blood sugar and the high effects of a sugar rush, but do we know that low blood sugar actually causes a release of cortisol – the 'stress' hormone? No wonder boys can't concentrate when they are hungry!

Fish oils

There is a consensus of opinion in favour of fish oils to help children's concentration, and this is again particularly effective with boys. Michael Gurian (2001) helps to explain this as 'The human brain is just over 60% fat and requires omega 3 acids to promote optimal brain performance'.

One brand of fish oil commissioned research in Durham Schools into 'the effect of fatty acid supplementation on the behaviour and learning of primary school-age children'. The results showed that children taking these fish oils:

- generally had better behaviour – with marked improvements in hyperactivity, inattention and impulsivity
- had highly significant improvements in short-term auditory memory which is known to have a profound impact on learning ability and reading

Do these behaviours represent those we have been discussing as being more typical in boys, especially those with ADHD?

Margot Sunderland suggests that doctors should prescribe fish oils before they prescribe Ritalin or other drugs used for treating ADHD. She also raised my awareness to other key ingredients in a boy's diet.

Zinc

I was familiar with the link between testosterone and the need for zinc (HACSG) especially at stressful times, but I knew little of the effects of the emotion chemicals dopamine and serotonin.

Dopamine

Dopamine is one of the chemicals essential for coordination, drive, motivation and interest in learning. If it is lacking boys can feel lethargic, lazy, even depressed.

In order to maintain our dopamine levels we need to get tyrosine through eating protein. If we eat carbohydrate for breakfast it lasts us half an hour; if we eat protein it keeps us going for up to three hours. I suggest schools and families offer breakfasts with protein. The difference is quite striking. Boys, girls and the adults who care for them have much more tolerance, drive and as Margot Sunderland puts it . . . 'GO'.

Throughout this book, two of my greatest influences have been Margot Sunderland and Steve Biddulph. They have both, in different ways, shown me the importance of one final food. This simple natural food source has the potential to stave off: depression, irritability, anger, panic attacks, lethargy and impulsivity and of course hunger.

Serotonin

Serotonin is the chemical this food increases (through activating tryptophan) and that is crucial at times of high testosterone, especially in adolescence. It is a mood stabilizer and brings increased control to our impulses. Steve Biddulph asked for one when presenting at a conference; Margot Sunderland suggests we eat one to overcome bad behaviour or to help us sleep. . . . It is – the humble banana!

Conclusion: A brighter future for boys – changing lives

With schools, families and communities working together the future for boys has never been brighter. There is so much potential and passion enabling the people in the lives of boys to drive things forward, to make things better and to change lives. There is no question that in changing the future for boys we will change lives for everyone. You can no more change one leg of a table and expect the others to be unaffected than you can make positive changes to the life of a boy and not expect the family and all around him to benefit too.

Together we need to focus on the Big Issues for Boys:

FEAR	We need to turn the fear of boys and men into trust, respect, confidence and good relationships
BLAME	We need to lose the labels and blame culture so often directed at boys and men. We need to see the strengths, the successes and celebrate these. We need to turn away from blame and act with positive solutions
UNDERSTANDING	Male or female, parent or teacher, young or old . . . everyone needs to understand boys, where they are coming from and what they need in order for us to believe in them, value them and be proud of them
MENTORS	Boys need trusted men in their lives, they need real role models and supportive mentors. Boys need people who know how to guide each individual in how to become a good and successful man
PASSION	Boys need to have a passion and a purpose. They need to know what drives them and have determined people to support them and help to make it happen.

The way forward is simple . . . less stress, more passion.

Society is the major cause of stress, our society of extremes . . . No one seems to have a 'happy medium'. We need to learn from both extremes . . .

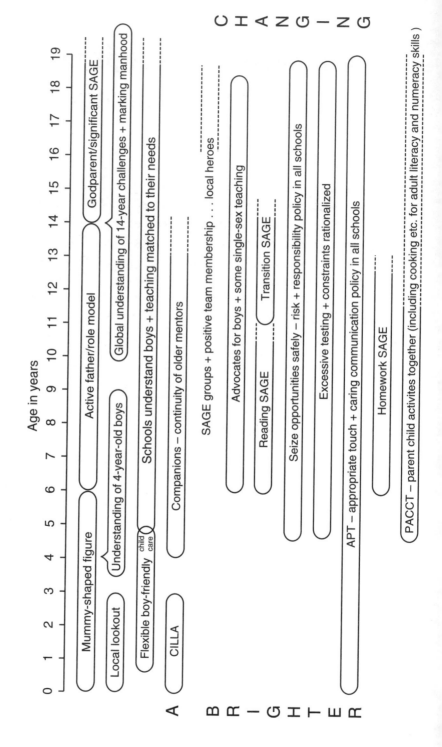

Age in years

0 1 2 3 4 5 6 7 8 9 10 11 12 13 14 15 16 17 18 19

A

Mummy-shaped figure | Active father/role model | Godparent/significant SAGE

Local lookout | Understanding of 4-year-old boys | Global understanding of 14-year challenges + marking manhood

Flexible boy-friendly child care | Schools understand boys + teaching matched to their needs

CILLA | Companions – continuity of older mentors

B R I G H T E R

SAGE groups + positive team membership . . . local heroes

Advocates for boys + some single-sex teaching

Reading SAGE | Transition SAGE

Seize opportunities safely – risk + responsibility policy in all schools

Excessive testing + constraints rationalized

APT – appropriate touch + caring communication policy in all schools

Homework SAGE

PACCT – parent child activites together (including cooking etc. for adult literacy and numeracy skills)

C H A N G - N G

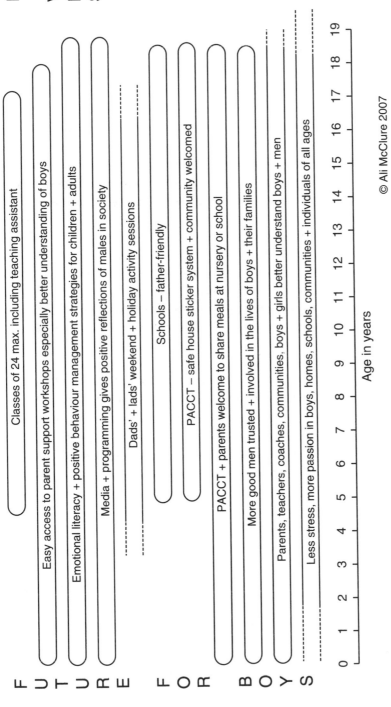

FUTURE FOR BOYS LIVES

Classes of 24 max. including teaching assistant

Easy access to parent support workshops especially better understanding of boys

Emotional literacy + positive behaviour management strategies for children + adults

Media + programming gives positive reflections of males in society

Dads' + lads' weekend + holiday activity sessions

Schools – father-friendly

PACCT – safe house sticker system + community welcomed

PACCT + parents welcome to share meals at nursery or school

More good men trusted + involved in the lives of boys + their families

Parents, teachers, coaches, communities, boys + girls better understand boys + men

Less stress, more passion in boys, homes, schools, communities + individuals of all ages

Age in years

0 1 2 3 4 5 6 7 8 9 10 11 12 13 14 15 16 17 18 19

© Ali McClure 2007

When families are in crisis, charities come to their aid and offer support. When families have sufficient money and too little time they buy in support. We need to make the best examples of this support available for every family, every member of the community, every boy.

Society into reality

We need to move on from the stresses of society and turn them into a purposeful, balanced reality. We need to hold on to our vision for LESS STRESS–MORE PASSION. As parents and teachers we need to find ways to overcome the stress for ourselves and to seek opportunities to help others overcome their stresses and find their passion. PACCT can help each one of us make that difference.

We can make things better through:

Passion	fuelled by what we have read and experienced
Understanding	from brain wiring, man as hunter and observing boys in action
Motivation	purpose – knowing specific changes each one of us can make
Action	make it happen, being the pebble in the pond, the mosquito in the bed

Less stress, more passion. . . .

Boys are, at best struggling, at worst simply surviving in our society and schools. Their future depends on good men and understanding women with a purpose and a passion. Those good men and understanding women are you and I.

If we believe in a bright future for all boys we *will* work together to . . .

Make things Better for Boys in schools, in families, in communities, in life!

Glossary

AAA	Allow Adapt Add – relating to behaviour
ABC–STUV	Anger Blame Condemnation Stop and Smile, Think and Talk, Understand, Value
ADD	Attention Deficit Disorder
ADHD	Attention Deficit Hyperactivity Disorder
Advocates for Boys	A person in a school, ideally of the same gender, to understand, promote and support the needs of boys
APT	Appropriate Physical Touch
ASBO	Anti-social Behaviour Orders (UK)
Brag Book	A book for boys to keep in order to recognize and share achievements
Break Buddy	A child who is chosen to 'walk and talk' with their teacher at breaktime
CCC	Caring Contact and Communication
CILLA	Continuity of Individual Love Learning and Attention
Companion	An older member of the community who becomes involved with young children in school, supporting them and sharing meals with them
ECM	Every Child Matters – A UK government green paper promoting the following outcomes for children and families with profound effects on schools to provide Extended Services. It led into the Children's Act 2004 and later the Children's Plan 2007

- Be healthy
- Stay safe
- Enjoy and achieve through learning
- Make a positive contribution to society
- Achieve economic well-being

Extended Schools	Schools which offer Extended Services to promote ECM outcomes
Extended Services	Services offered around schools to promote ECM outcomes
Family Links	A charity promoting emotional literacy, nurturing and relationship skills (UK)
FIX	Facts, 'I' Statement, X=fixing the problem together
Focus	A description of a task or support to help a child with a specific need
Focus Group	A group of children with the need to achieve a specific shared outcome or focus
GCSE	General Certificate of Secondary Education (UK)
HACSG	Hyperactive Children's Support Group. Charity to support Hyperactive Children and their families (UK)
Homestart	A UK charity to support young families
ICAN	Children's communication charity (UK)
KAVES	Kinaesthetic, Auditory, Visual, Emotional, Sensory
Local Heroes	Local Role models sharing their achievements
Local Lookout	A local person to support and look out for expectant mums and young families
NCH	National Children's Homes – Charity (UK)
NCT	National Childbirth Trust – a childbirth and parenting charity
NEET	Not in Education, Employment or Training
PACCT	Parents Adults Children Communities and Teachers – Group of people affiliated to a school to help promote the aims of Every Child Matters
Projects with a Purpose	A way to organize the curriculum to promote learning with real purpose
PUMA	Passion, Understanding, Motivation, Action
R and R	Risk and Responsibility
Reading SAGE	A SAGE who works with a child to help them learn to read and to promote a love of reading

SAGE	Same gender mentor, also describes a person of wisdom
SAGE group	A group of same-sex children who meet regularly with a SAGE
SAGE homework	Specific, fun homework set for a boy to do with his father or same-sex mentor
SATS	Standard Assessment Tests at ages 7, 11 and 14 (UK)
Social Responsibility Policy	Policy promoted within business to promote Social Responsibility and a commitment to support their local community
SPADE	Specific, Proud, Authentic, Descriptive Emotional – to describe methods of praise
The Home Environment	A way to organize a nursery setting to promote CILLA
UNICEF	United Nations Children's Fund – Charity to protect children worldwide
VAK	Visual, Auditory, Kinaesthetic – Styles of Learning

References

Armitage, R and Armitage, D (1994) *The Lighthouse Keeper's Lunch*, London: Scholastic

Baron-Cohen, S (2003) *The Essential Difference*, London: Penguin

Biddulph, S (1994) *Manhood: An Action Plan for Changing Men's Lives*, Stroud: Hawthorn Press

Biddulph, S (1998) *Raising Boys: Why Boys are Different and How to Help Them Become Happy and Well-balanced Men*, London: Thorsons (HarperCollins)

Biddulph, S (2005) *Raising Babies: Should Under 3s Go to Nursery?* London: Thorsons (HarperCollins)

Brizendine, MD, L (2006) *The Female Brain*, London: Bantam Press

Cresswell, C (2003) *Mathematics and Sex*, NSW Australia: Allen & Unwin

Daly, T (2005) *How to Turn Any Disruptive Child Into Your Best Student*, USA: Smarty Pants www.adhdsolution.com, last accessed date 12 December 2007

De Botton, A (2005) *Status Anxiety All You Need is Status*, London: Penguin

Freed, J, M.A.T. and Parsons, L (1997) *Right-Brained Children in a Left-Brained World: Unlocking the Potential of Your ADD Child*, New York, USA: Fireside (Simon & Schuster)

Gurian, M (2001) *Boys and Girls Learn Differently: A Guide for Teachers and Parents*, San Francisco, USA: Jossey-Bass

Gurian, M and Steven, K (2005) *The Minds of Boys: Saving Our Sons From Falling Behind in School and Life*, San Francisco, USA: Jossey-Bass

Hannaford, C and Pert, C (2005) *Smart Moves: Why Learning Is not all in Your Head*, California, USA: The Learning Gym, Manhattan Beach

Hemery, D (2005) *How to Help Children Find the Champion within Themselves*, London: BBC

Hunt,C and Mountford, A (2003) *The Parenting Puzzle: How to Get the Best out of Family Life*, Oxford: Family Links

Kagan, J (1994) *The Nature of the Child*, New York, USA: Basic Books (Perseus)

Kimura, D (2000) *Sex and Cognition*, Massachusettes, USA: Massachusetts Institute of Technology

Lucas, B (2005) *Discover Your Hidden Talents*, Stafford, Network Educational Press

Macmillan, Dr B (2004) *Why Boys are Different and how to Bring out the Best in Them*, London: Octopus (Hamlyn)

Manolson, A, Ward, B and Dodington, N (2007) *You Make the Difference: In Helping Your Child Learn*, Toronto, Canada: Thistle

McBride Dabbs, J with Godwin Dabbs, M (2000) *Heroes, Rogues and Lovers: Testosterone and Behaviour*, New York, USA: McGraw-Hill

Moir, A and Jessel, D (1991) *Brain Sex: The Real Difference Between Men and Women*, New York, USA: Dell Publishing

Ortberg, J (2001) *If You Want to Walk on Water You've Got to Get Out of the Boat*, Michigan, USA: Zonderman Publishing

Palmer, S(2006) *Toxic Childhood: How the Modern World Is Damaging Our Children and What We Can Do About It*, London: Orion

Pease, A and Pease, B (1991) *Why Men Don't Listen and Women Can't Read Maps: How We're Different and What To Do About It*, London: Orion

Siegel, G, Albers, W, Katzman, R, and Agranoff, B(1976) *Basic NeuroChemistry*, Boston, USA: Little Brown and Company

Sieger, R (2006) 42 *Days to Wealth, Health and Happiness: How to Take Control and Transform Your Life Forever*, London: Arrow Books (Random House)

Sunderland, M (2006) *The Science of Parenting: Practical Guidance on Sleep, Crying, Play and Building Emotional Well Being for Life*, London: Dorling Kindersley (Penguin)

Useful websites

www.adhdsolution.com (Tom Daly) (last accessed 12 December 2007)

www.barnados.org.uk/babyfather (last accessed 12 December 2007)

www.braingym.org.uk (last accessed 12 December 2007)

www.dfes.gov.uk (Children are unbeatable alliance) (last accessed 12 December 2007)

www.eoc.org.uk (The Gender Agenda) (last accessed 12 December 2007)

www.essilor.co.uk (last accessed 12 December 2007)

www.familylinks.org.uk (The Nurturing Programme) (last accessed 12 December 2007)

www.fathersdirect.com (The Nurturing Programme) (last accessed 12 December 2007)

www.fnf.org.uk (Families need Fathers) (last accessed 12 December 2007)

www.hacsg.org.uk (Hyperactive Children's Support Group) (last accessed 12 December 2007)

www.hanen.org (helping your child to learn) (last accessed 12 December 2007)

www.home-start.org.uk (last accessed 12 December 2007)

www.ican.org.uk (children's communication charity) (last accessed 12 December 2007)

www.jollylearning.co.uk (Jolly phonics) (last accessed 12 December 2007)

www.jrf.org.uk (Joseph Rowntree Foundation – social policy research) (last accessed 12 December 2007)

www.mediasmart.org.uk (last accessed 12 December 2007)

www.mibfb.com (Making It Better for Boys) (will become live on 1 June 2008)

www.nct.org.uk (National Childbirth Trust) (last accessed 12 December 2007)

www.outoftheark.com (last accessed 12 December 2007)

www.outwardbound.org.uk (adventurous activities) (last accessed 12 December 2007)

www.compassonline.org.uk (last accessed 12 December 2007)

www.parenting-forum.org.uk (last accessed 12 December 2007)

www.respect.gov.uk (respect agenda) (last accessed 12 December 2007)

www.savethechildren.org.uk (last accessed 12 December 2007)

www.surreycafis.org.uk (Dads and Lads) (last accessed 12 December 2007)

Index